KAREN MARTINI began her food career at the age of fifteen at Mietta's in Melbourne. She worked at various restaurants before taking the helm at the Melbourne Wine Room, which has proved a resounding and enduring success for her ever since. In 2002 she moved to Sydney to take up the position of Executive Chef at Icebergs Dining Room and Bar – a meeting of Melbourne style and Sydney glamour. On her return to Melbourne, Karen and her husband Michael Sapountsis opened mr wolf, a chic pizzeria in St Kilda. Karen is food editor of *Sunday Life* magazine and food presenter on the television show *Better Homes and Gardens*. Karen Martini's two previous cookbooks are *Where the Heart Is* and *Cooking at Home*.

karenmartini.com

FOR MICHAEL,
STELLA AND AMBER

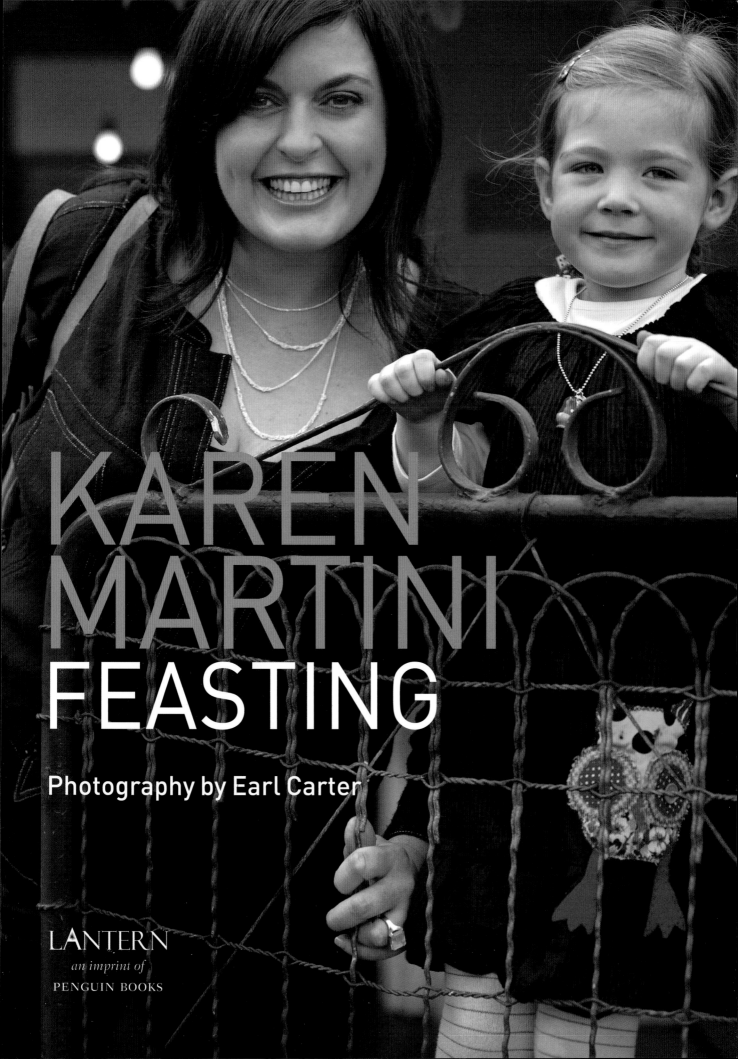

KAREN MARTINI
FEASTING

Photography by Earl Carter

LANTERN
an imprint of
PENGUIN BOOKS

CONTENTS

QUICK RECIPE GUIDE

TO START

Bruschetta with smashed broad beans, garlic
and parmesan 53

Crostini with chicken liver and cannellini
bean pate 30

Domatokeftedes 182

Egg and silverbeet wrap with feta and dukkah 237

Fried egg in brik pastry with caper and parsley salad
and hot chilli sauce 256

Ham and potato frittata with witlof relish 232

Labna and Tunisian dukkah with pickled spring
vegetables 114

Oysters with smoked herring roe and spring
onion dressing 16

Potato focaccia with anchovies and caramelised
onion 62

Prawn and parsley mayonnaise on toasted
baguette 279

Ricotta and feta fritters with walnuts and
yoghurt sauce 131

Ricotta tarts with cured ocean trout 230

Spinach, zucchini and pea fritters with prawns
and preserved lemon dressing 260

Sweet and sour dried figs on pan-fried
haloumi 184

Tuna carpaccio with parsley, almond and
hard-boiled egg 6

Watercress, pea and potato soup with crumbed
oysters 158

Yoghurt, green chilli and mint dip with fried
beans and paprika 184

Za'atar-dusted ricotta and haloumi pastries with
pomegranate molasses 150

SEAFOOD

Barbecued octopus 189

Barbounia baked with fennel, capers and
lemon 23

Blue eye with fried butter beans and garlic
and sour lemon dressing 77

Calamari and bulgur salad with mint, chilli
and asparagus 220

Calamari seared with potato, radicchio and
fried breadcrumbs 66

Coriander and oyster omelette 173

Flathead and potato fishcakes 74

Mussels fried with tomato, black pepper
and fennel seeds 35

Ocean trout fillet with mint labna 279

Pan-fried prawns with green chilli sauce 54

Pork and prawn dumplings with shiitake
and ginger 168

Prawn and watermelon salad with feta, mint
and pomegranate 140

Rolled sardine fillets baked with vine leaves
and tomato 185

Salt and pepper squid 169

Snapper, scallop, clam and potato pie 255

Snapper spiced with baharat and garlic 262

Sour-cream pastry tart with smoked trout
and caramelised onion 241

CHICKEN AND OTHER BIRDS

Noodles with roast duck and hoisin sauce 176

Pan-roasted chicken legs with parsnip skordalia 37

Roast chicken stuffed with parsley, hazelnuts
and butter 106

Roast chicken with coriander seeds, thyme and
cherry tomatoes 151

Roast chicken with shredded spinach and yoghurt 210

Roast duck with rhubarb and ginger relish 272

Roast spatchcock with chorizo, tomato and yellow
pea paste 163

Soba noodle salad with broccoli, chicken and
toasted nori 219

Spiced chicken, quail and pistachio terrine 283

Thai-inspired lime and chicken bean thread noodles 177

Turkish chicken with apricots, saffron and pistachios 145

MEAT

Beef shiskabob 122

Chargrilled scotch fillet with summer herbed oil,
ricotta and lemon 69

Crispy fried lamb with chickpea puree and carrot
and beetroot salad 141

Green egg and pancetta puff-pastry pie 245

Ham hock, red lentil and tomato broth 206

Ham hock terrine with parsley and lentils 269

Pork and prawn dumplings with shiitake and ginger 168

Roast rack of lamb with capsicum, tomatoes on the
vine and smashed broad beans 79

Saba-glazed ham with pickled cherries 290

Scrambled eggs with chorizo and spring onions 245

Seared eye fillet with porcini dressing 56

Sesame beef with spring onions, green chilli and
brown rice 223

Slow-baked lamb shoulder 192

Slow-cooked lamb with potato and barley 8

Slow-roasted pork belly with cucumber, coriander
and sesame-spiced dressing 179

Spicy Lebanese-style peas with minced lamb 122

GREENS

Avocado with sprouts and umeboshi plum
dressing 219

Baby potatoes with sour cream, pistachios
and dill 153

Bagna cauda with soft-boiled eggs and asparagus 76

Baked beans with mustard seeds, vinegar
and tomato 251

Baked potatoes with sour cream, horseradish
and burnt butter 56

Beetroot slaw with apple and red cabbage 209

Braised peas with anchovies, garlic, mint and
potatoes 21

Broad beans with garlic and harissa 153

Celery, parsley and lemon salad 9

Chargrilled asparagus with cherry tomatoes
and buffalo mozzarella 240

Creamed spinach 107

Freekah salad with feta, toasted almonds, lemon
and parsley 192

Fresh tomato and lime chutney 262

Marouli salad 196

Northern Italian olive mill soup 44

Orange, tomato and parsley salad with celery seeds
and green chilli 159

Red kidney bean and capsicum hotpot 133

Ricotta, baby spinach, witlof and fresh peas 47

Ricotta salata with tomatoes, onion and basil 69

Roast parsnip with white sweet potato 271

Simple potato dauphinoise 107

Slow-cooked zucchini with tomato, lemon and
coriander dressing 196

Smoked eggplant soup with feta bruschetta, cumin
and coriander oil 132

Spiral broccoli with brown butter, anchovies
and pine nuts 38

Steamed eggplant with black vinegar and shiitake 177

Stir-fried asparagus with tofu, wombok and
almonds 174

Tunisian carrot and potato salad with egg, green chilli
and capers 121

Zaalouk (slow-cooked eggplant and tomato salad) 117

PASTA AND RICE

Koushary 261
Orecchiette with parsley, almond paste, vongole
    and chorizo 21
Orzo with crayfish, peas and sorrel 287
Quinoa, rice and tomato pilav 123
Trofie with prawns, leek, lemon and bottarga 271
Truffled mozzarella arancini 31

SWEETS

Almond and clove baklava with citrus
    syrup 203
Campari and blood orange jellies with vanilla
    ice-cream 80
Cherry and almond burnt-butter torte 70
Cherry, raspberry and vanilla jam 275
Chianti and raspberry granita with vanilla
    ice-cream 12
Chocolate and banana loaf 249
Chocolate and beetroot brownies 246
Chocolate and orange creme caramel 110
Chocolate mousse and hazelnut meringue
    cake 48
Chocolate mousse with coffee granita 200
Chocolate roulade with marmalade
    ice-cream 40
Choux ring with raisin cream and toffee
    sauce 297
Coconut butter cake with passionfruit icing 93
Cold citrus souffle with raspberry toffee
    sauce 275
Crostoli knots with honey, orange blossom
    and sesame 88
Crushed honeycomb and fromage frais
    panna cotta 164
Free-form peach tart 224
Ginger lemonade with Angostura bitters 229
Hokey pokey rocky road 88

Honeycomb 164
Layered crepe cake with walnut jam and
    chocolate ganache 94
Moroccan mess 126
Moroccan semolina pancakes with honeycomb
    butter and banana 239
Nougat cassata 292
Pineapple tossed in shredded coconut with
    mango and blueberries 229
Poached apricots with orange blossom cream
    and apple verbena jelly 154
Raspberry-iced cupcakes 101
Rhubarb and raspberry tarts 58
Ricotta on toast with figs and honey 246
Sherry and cherry trifle 294
Slow-baked apple pie 256
Sour cherry and ricotta strudel 84
Sticky ginger and pear cake 98
Super-rich chocolate and chestnut mousse
    cake 26
Sweet quinoa with dried apricots, almonds
    and orange blossom water 136
Toffee-dipped dates stuffed with almonds and
    chocolate 146
Watermelon and raspberry salad with rosewater
    and yoghurt sorbet 264
Yoghurt, honey and chocolate cake 215

INTRODUCTION

This is a book about how to celebrate, how to come together around a table. I cook in my restaurants, on television and for my weekly magazine articles, but the thing I love most is cooking at home for family and friends. If I don't have a special occasion to celebrate, I make one up: the middle of summer, the end of winter, the start of the broad-bean season – any excuse will do.

Like many other families, we celebrate all our special occasions with a feast. Because we have people around so much, I tend not to think in terms of single dishes – so often it's about multiple plates at the centre of a shared table. Pulling together a meal does require a little thought and planning, but it is also an act of love. And when all the moving parts come together, it's a wonderfully creative and satisfying process.

At book signings, the questions people ask me all come back to one theme: how to make all the parts of a meal work together. 'What can I serve for dessert if I am having risotto as a main?'; 'Is it okay to have a seafood entree and main course?'; and 'What can I cook for a formal dinner?'.

There are so many cookbooks out there and lots of cooking shows, and as a result the number of great home cooks is on the rise. People have the confidence to experiment with different flavours and cooking methods, but there is still a lot of uncertainty about how to match flavours across a meal; how to get the balance right so the entire meal isn't dominated by one set of flavours or type of produce (for example, too heavy on carbs or dairy) – or by a clash of flavours and textures.

This is why *Feasting* is organised the way it is. Rather than use traditional chapter headings, such as Starters and Mains, I have grouped dishes into menus. I have designed these menus with the following things in mind.

What's important when planning a meal?

The first is season. This is so important. Even if you can get tomatoes in July (which you can) you don't want to make them the centrepiece of your meal because they just won't have the flavour. An example of a great seasonal menu in this book is the Winter Lunch. We start with oysters, which are always better in winter, served with smoked herring roe. The pasta course is orecchiette, which is warm and filling. The main course is barbounia and that great winter vegetable staple, fennel. And the dessert is a super-rich chocolate mousse cake – definitely one you wouldn't serve during the warmer months.

The next thing to consider is whether a menu is suitable to the occasion and the time you have available. Spending days on a big Christmas lunch with all the trimmings is right for that time of the year, especially when there are people around to help out. But if you are hosting a simple weekend lunch with friends, you need to choose a menu that won't keep you in the kitchen all afternoon. The Simple Sunday menu is great for easy entertaining. There is a roast chook (everyone's favourite) which can be stuffed the night before; the creme caramel dessert can also be made the day before; and the potatoes can be peeled early in the day and kept in a pan of water. All you have to do when it's time to eat is slice and cook the potatoes and make the creamed spinach.

The cuisine background is a great organising theme for any meal. You can certainly tweak the recipes, but if you use the basic flavour palate of a specific cuisine in all the dishes, you'll be able to cook with confidence. A great example of this is my dad's mother, who is from Tunisia. She may have only twelve dishes in her repertoire, but I have created so many different interpretations just by using the base spices she relies on.

Recently I've been focusing on Greek and Moroccan flavours, and you'll see the results of this when flicking through the book. I don't cook Asian-style food in my restaurants, but I love cooking it at home. The Asian Banquet I have included is a mix of Thai and Chinese food. The menu includes moreish steamed dumplings, salt and pepper squid (which I always order at restaurants), stir-fried asparagus and pork belly with a sesame-spiced dressing that features tahini, creating an unusual flavour combination.

The fourth thing I give a lot of thought to when planning a menu is texture. This is an element that is often overlooked, but you don't want all the dishes on the table to be creamy, or crunchy, or chewy – you need to offer a little bit of everything. In the Family Winter Dinner, for example, I start with a cold fish dish, which is silky, then move to a rich, unctuous slow-cooked lamb, which is served with an astringent celery salad that cuts through the fat of the meat. To finish it all off, there's a wonderfully granular granita.

Practicalities

Please don't feel that you have to cook every dish included in a particular menu. Some of them have a lot of recipes – just look at the Big Brunch Celebration! If you were having forty people over for a christening you might consider cooking the entire menu, but if it's just a few friends on a Sunday morning, three or four dishes should be enough. Similarly, The Greek Feast has eleven recipes but a selection of, say, five dishes would work beautifully on a warm summer's evening.

If you are fairly new to cooking, start with a couple of dishes at a time and build up from there. Focus first on researching and shopping for ingredients. I have a few golden shopping rules: get to know your suppliers; think about where the food is coming from; where possible, buy produce that has been produced locally; and eggs and chicken should always be organic.

When you're working your way through a menu, read the instructions all the way through, look for any preparation that can be done in advance, and see which tasks can be done in tandem. If you're planning a big event with friends or family, clearly divide up the elements of the menu so you don't end up with three potato salads instead of a well-balanced feast.

Don't feel locked into the menus in this book. To make cooking across menus easy, we have included two contents lists: one simply gives the menu titles, while the other lists all the dishes under traditional headings such as Seafood, Greens and Desserts.

Most of all, enjoy

My husband Michael's family is Greek. They have a state-of-the-art six-burner stove in the kitchen, but they cook everything outside! That's how they love to celebrate.

This is what this book is all about: making it easier to celebrate in a way that suits you. Some readers will delight in spending three days in the kitchen preparing the Christmas Buffet Extravaganza, while others will find a few recipes they can put together quickly.

And don't forget the kids. My two little ones taste everything and we all eat together at least three times a week. It's a source of great joy for us.

For me, cooking is one of life's great pleasures and a hugely creative endeavour, but food is not an end in itself. Food's true wonder is that it gives us an opportunity for conversation, connection and celebration. If you can use this book to help create a sense of occasion and delight at mealtimes, if it makes the idea of entertaining a little easier, if it allows you to get together more often with your favourite people, then I'll consider my job well done.

Get cooking and happy feasting!

FAMILY WINTER DINNER

TUNA CARPACCIO WITH PARSLEY,
ALMOND AND HARD-BOILED EGG

SLOW-COOKED LAMB WITH POTATO AND BARLEY

CELERY, PARSLEY AND LEMON SALAD

CHIANTI AND RASPBERRY GRANITA
WITH VANILLA ICE-CREAM

500 g piece yellowfin tuna
sea salt and freshly ground black pepper
2 slices sourdough bread
1 clove garlic, peeled
¼ bunch flat-leaf parsley, leaves picked
¼ bunch mint, leaves picked
30 g toasted almonds, chopped
½ red onion, finely diced
120 ml extra virgin olive oil
2 lemons
3 hard-boiled eggs, sliced

TUNA CARPACCIO WITH PARSLEY, ALMOND AND HARD-BOILED EGG

Carpaccio is a seductive starter or light lunch. To get the most out of this simple dish, make sure all of your ingredients are the freshest available.

Slice the tuna by hand as thinly as possible and arrange on a chilled platter. Season well with salt and pepper.

Toast or grill the bread slices then rub with the garlic clove. Tear into small pieces.

Combine the bread, parsley, mint, almonds, onion and 2 tablespoons olive oil in a bowl. Season to taste, then set aside for 10 minutes.

Cut one lemon in half and squeeze the juice into a small bowl. Remove the skin and pith from the second lemon and cut it into segments and then into small triangles.

Arrange the egg slices over the tuna slices and scatter with the bread and herb mixture and lemon segments.

Combine the lemon juice with the remaining olive oil and drizzle over the tuna and salad. Serve immediately.

3 tablespoons extra virgin olive oil

50 g butter

900 g boned lamb shoulder (including the neck),
    cut into 4–5 cm chunks

sea salt and freshly ground black pepper

18 golden shallots, peeled

8 cloves garlic, sliced

1 bunch dutch (baby) carrots,
    peeled and trimmed

1 bay leaf

5 sprigs thyme

4 juniper berries

4 waxy potatoes, peeled and
    cut into 5 mm thick slices

140 g fine pearl barley

grated zest and juice of 1 orange

grated zest and juice of 1 lemon

2 vegetable stock cubes

1 small bunch cavolo nero, washed,
    thick veins removed

SLOW-COOKED LAMB WITH POTATO AND BARLEY

This is a simple, thrown-together dish with fabulous
flavours, where all the magic happens in the oven.
It is divinely hearty on a cold winter's day.

Preheat the oven to 170°C (fan-forced).

Heat the olive oil and half the butter in a heavy-based
casserole dish over high heat. Add the lamb chunks
(in batches if necessary) and brown well, then season
with salt and pepper and remove from the pan.

Add the shallots and garlic and cook for a few minutes
until softened and slightly coloured. Stir in the carrots,
herbs and remaining butter and cook for 1 minute.
Add the potato, barley and the orange and lemon zest
and juice and mix well, then crumble in the stock cubes.
Return the lamb to the pan and cover with water. Bring
the mixture to the boil, then top with the cavolo nero
leaves. Cover and cook in the oven for about 2 hours
or until the lamb is tender and the potato has broken
down into the juices.

Pictured page 10.

SERVES 6–8

½ small head cauliflower, broken into small florets
170 ml extra virgin olive oil
2 hearts of celery, sliced, leaves picked and reserved
2 teaspoons salt flakes
2 teaspoons sugar
2 green chillies, sliced
2 large lemons, segmented, juice squeezed
　from the middle and reserved
2 spring onions, finely sliced
1 bunch flat-leaf parsley, leaves picked
½ bunch watercress, leaves picked and chopped
sea salt and freshly ground black pepper

CELERY, PARSLEY AND LEMON SALAD

This wonderfully astringent salad complements the richness of the braised lamb and refreshes the palate. It would also be lovely with pan-fried fish fillets and mashed potato.

Preheat the oven to 200°C (fan-forced).

Toss the cauliflower florets with 2½ tablespoons olive oil in a bowl. Transfer to a baking tray and roast for 25 minutes or until golden. Remove and set aside to cool to room temperature.

Meanwhile, place the celery in a shallow bowl and sprinkle with the salt and sugar. Leave it for 20 minutes to soften, then squeeze out any excess moisture.

In a large bowl, combine the chilli, lemon segments and juice, and 3 tablespoons olive oil. Add the spring onion, parsley, watercress, celery, celery leaves and cauliflower and gently toss. Season with salt and pepper, then allow to rest for 10 minutes.

Drizzle the remaining olive oil over the salad and serve.

Pictured page 11.

Slow-cooked lamb with potato and barley (see page 8)

Celery, parsley and lemon salad (see page 9)

400 ml chianti

120 ml water

80 g caster sugar

2 teaspoons liquid glucose

2 strips lemon zest

250 g raspberries (fresh or frozen)

1 litre good-quality vanilla ice-cream

CHIANTI AND RASPBERRY GRANITA WITH VANILLA ICE-CREAM

Use a chianti you enjoy drinking for this icy dessert, as the wine flavour is reasonably prominent.

Place the chianti, water, sugar, glucose and lemon zest in a small stainless-steel saucepan. Simmer over high heat for 3–4 minutes, then remove from the heat and allow to cool slightly. Strain through a sieve into a shallow 30 cm × 15 cm dish and scatter the raspberries over the top.

Freeze for 4–6 hours, then use a fork to break up the granita. Return the dish to the freezer until you're ready to serve. (You can make the granita up to 2 days before you need it and store it, covered, in the freezer.)

Chill serving glasses in the freezer for 10 minutes. Place a scoop of vanilla ice-cream in each glass, then top with the granita and serve immediately.

WINTER LUNCH

OYSTERS WITH SMOKED HERRING
ROE AND SPRING ONION DRESSING

ORECCHIETTE WITH PARSLEY, ALMOND
PASTE, VONGOLE AND CHORIZO

BRAISED PEAS WITH ANCHOVIES,
GARLIC, MINT AND POTATOES

BARBOUNIA BAKED WITH
FENNEL, CAPERS AND LEMON

SUPER-RICH CHOCOLATE AND
CHESTNUT MOUSSE CAKE

SERVES 4

1 head curly endive, outer leaves separated and washed
12 Pacific oysters, freshly shucked (keep the lids
   to lay on the platter)
30 g black, slightly smoked herring roe
lemon wedges, to serve
thinly sliced rye bread, to serve

Spring onion dressing
juice of ½ lemon
1½ tablespoons extra virgin olive oil
1 tablespoon sherry vinegar
2–3 spring onions, finely sliced
freshly ground black pepper

OYSTERS WITH SMOKED HERRING ROE AND SPRING ONION DRESSING

I tried oysters with a simple smoked roe dressing at a tapas bar recently – they were the inspiration for this recipe. Lumpfish roe is available from speciality food stores or the deli section of some supermarkets. If you want to pull out all the stops, use caviar instead – it's spectacular in this recipe.

To make the dressing, combine all the ingredients in a small bowl. Set aside.

Blanch the endive in salted boiling water for 2 minutes. Drain and refresh under cold water, then squeeze out any excess liquid using a clean tea towel.

Spread the endive on a platter with the reserved oyster lids and arrange the oysters on top. Spoon a little roe onto each oyster and serve the dressing in a separate bowl so everyone can add their own. Serve immediately with lemon wedges and rye bread.

Orecchiette with parsley, almond paste,
vongole and chorizo (see page 21)

SERVES 4

50 g roasted almonds, chopped

4 small cloves garlic, peeled

2 teaspoons sea salt, or to taste

½ bunch flat-leaf parsley, leaves picked and finely chopped

140 ml extra virgin olive oil

350 g orecchiette pasta

150 g hot chorizo sausage, chopped

800 g vongole, washed thoroughly in cold water

120 ml dry white wine

100 ml pouring cream

sea salt and freshly ground black pepper

< ORECCHIETTE WITH PARSLEY, ALMOND PASTE, VONGOLE AND CHORIZO

The combination of chorizo, parsley, vongole and almonds may sound a bit crazy, but you must trust me. It is a sublime mix.

Crush the almonds and 1 clove garlic with the salt in a mortar and pestle. Gradually add the parsley and 2 tablespoons olive oil and pound to a coarse paste. Slice the remaining garlic.

Cook the pasta in plenty of lightly salted boiling water until al dente.

Meanwhile, cook the chorizo in a large saucepan or flat-bottomed wok over high heat for 2–3 minutes. Add the sliced garlic and vongole, then cover and steam for 4–5 minutes. Remove the pan from the heat and take out three-quarters of the vongole shells. Remove the meat from the shells and return it to the pan, then stir in the almond paste, white wine and remaining olive oil and simmer for 30 seconds.

Drain the pasta and add it to the pan, along with the cream. Stir well, then season to taste with salt and pepper and add more olive oil, if necessary. Serve immediately.

SERVES 4–6

6 large kipfler potatoes

460 g broad beans

120 ml extra virgin olive oil

8 anchovies

3 cloves garlic, sliced

4 golden shallots, finely sliced

2½ cups (300 g) frozen peas (fresh would also be great)

½ bunch flat-leaf parsley, leaves picked and chopped

2 tablespoons water

sea salt and freshly ground black pepper

5 sprigs mint, leaves picked and torn

juice of ½ lemon

BRAISED PEAS WITH ANCHOVIES, GARLIC, MINT AND POTATOES

This is the perfect side dish to accompany rare roast beef, barbecued lamb cutlets, or grilled or baked fish.

Cook the potatoes in lightly salted boiling water for 20 minutes until tender, then drain. When the potatoes are cool enough to handle, peel them and cut them into thick slices.

Meanwhile, blanch the broad beans in boiling water, then drain and double-peel them.

Heat the olive oil in a large frying pan over low heat. Cook the anchovies for about 1 minute, then add the garlic and shallot and cook for 2–3 minutes until lightly browned. Add the peas, parsley and water and cook over medium heat for 4–5 minutes. Season, then stir in the potato slices and broad beans and simmer for 2 minutes until warmed through. Finish with the mint and lemon juice and serve.

Pictured page 25.

1 bulb fennel

4 × 200 g red mullets, cleaned

sea salt and freshly ground black pepper

about 400 ml extra virgin olive oil

1 large lemon

6 large cloves garlic, thinly sliced

2 teaspoons fennel seeds, lightly crushed

2 handfuls fennel fronds or flat-leaf parsley leaves, torn

2 tablespoons capers

1¼ tablespoons red wine vinegar

1 egg white, lightly whisked

BARBOUNIA BAKED WITH FENNEL, CAPERS AND LEMON

Baking in paper is an easy way to cook whole fish such as red mullet (barbounia in Greek). I love to sear the little morsels in a hot pan to give a deeper flavour to the delicate fish before wrapping them up.

Boil the fennel bulb in a saucepan of salted water for about 30 minutes until tender. Drain and cut into small wedges.

Pat the fish cavities dry with paper towel, season well with salt and pepper and drizzle with 1–2 tablespoons olive oil.

Preheat the oven to 200°C (fan-forced). Tear off four 45 cm lengths of baking paper and set aside.

Cut the lemon in half, then slice one half and reserve the other half for juice. Set aside.

Heat about 300 ml olive oil in a large non-stick frying pan over medium heat (the oil should be about 1 cm deep). Add the garlic and cook for 2 minutes or until lightly golden, then throw in the fennel seeds. Immediately pour off the oil, garlic and seeds and reserve for later.

Increase the heat to high and add a generous splash of olive oil to the pan. Quickly fry the mullets for about 40 seconds on each side. Remove the fish from the pan and place each one on a piece of baking paper. (Depending on the size of your pan, you may need to do this in batches.)

Place some fennel fronds or parsley under each fish and season with salt. Divide the lemon slices and fennel wedges among the fish cavities and on top, then sprinkle with the capers. Pour over the reserved oil, seeds and fried garlic, a splash of vinegar and a squeeze of lemon juice.

Using a pastry brush, paint a crescent shape with egg white on one edge of the baking paper. Join the edges of paper to enclose the fish, then fold the edge over to make a curved parcel. Repeat with the remaining fish and paper.

Place the parcels on a large baking tray and bake for 12 minutes or until the fish is cooked. Rest for a minute, then serve in the bag. Rip the top open just before eating.

SERVES 8

285 g dark chocolate buttons

600 ml pouring cream

6 large egg yolks

170 g caster sugar

200 g canned unsweetened chestnut puree

2 tablespoons Marsala

2 tablespoons brandy

2 tablespoons cocoa powder, plus extra to serve

10 amaretti biscuits, crushed

creme fraiche, to serve

Marsala syrup

150 ml Marsala

100 g caster sugar

splash of brandy, to taste

SUPER-RICH CHOCOLATE AND CHESTNUT MOUSSE CAKE

One sliver of this mousse cake will be enough for even the most hardcore of chocolate lovers. The good news is that it only improves with age, so you can enjoy the leftovers for several days.

Preheat the oven to 130°C (fan-forced). Place a greased 25 cm tart tin on a baking tray.

Melt the chocolate in a heatproof bowl over a pan of barely simmering water (don't let the bowl touch the water) or in the microwave. Allow to cool slightly, then gradually stir in the cream until smooth.

Combine the egg yolks and sugar in a medium bowl and whisk until pale and smooth. Add the chestnut puree, Marsala and brandy and whisk until smooth, then stir in the cocoa powder.

Pour the chocolate mixture onto the yolks and stir until smooth. Pour the mixture into the prepared tin and bake for 45 minutes or until just set. Remove and cool to room temperature, then refrigerate for at least 2 hours before serving.

To make the syrup, combine the Marsala and sugar in a small saucepan and boil for 2 minutes until the sugar has dissolved. Add a splash of brandy.

Carefully turn the mousse out of the tin onto a serving plate. Press the amaretti biscuit crumbs onto the edges and dust over the extra cocoa. Pour the syrup over the top. Cut into slices and serve with creme fraiche.

SPECIAL ITALIAN WINTER DINNER

CROSTINI WITH CHICKEN LIVER
AND CANNELLINI BEAN PATE

TRUFFLED MOZZARELLA ARANCINI

MUSSELS FRIED WITH TOMATO,
BLACK PEPPER AND FENNEL SEEDS

PAN-ROASTED CHICKEN LEGS
WITH PARSNIP SKORDALIA

SPIRAL BROCCOLI WITH BROWN
BUTTER, ANCHOVIES AND PINE NUTS

CHOCOLATE ROULADE WITH
MARMALADE ICE-CREAM

SERVES 4

350 g free-range chicken livers,
   trimmed of white sinew
milk, for soaking
4 sprigs sage, large leaves picked
150 ml extra virgin olive oil
50 g butter
4 golden shallots, finely diced
4 cloves garlic, finely diced
sea salt and freshly ground black pepper
2 anchovies, chopped
4 sprigs thyme, leaves picked and chopped
5 sprigs sage, extra, leaves picked and chopped
2 tablespoons saba, plus extra to serve
400 g can cannellini beans, drained and rinsed,
   then crushed with the back of a spoon
1 small baguette, sliced and lightly toasted

CROSTINI WITH CHICKEN LIVER AND CANNELLINI BEAN PATE

This quick, gutsy pate is delicious with drinks or as a light starter. The cannellini beans absorb the juices from the livers and the saba. For those unfamiliar with saba, it is a type of sweet vinegar and is available from delis and specialist food stores.

Soak the livers in milk for 20 minutes to purge them of bitterness. Drain and cut in half, then dry them on paper towel.

Fry the sage leaves in 100 ml olive oil until golden. Remove and drain on paper towel.

Heat half the remaining olive oil and half the butter in a large frying pan over medium heat. Add the shallot and garlic and cook for 4 minutes or until soft, then add the remaining butter. Increase the heat to high. Add the livers and cook on one side for 2 minutes, then turn and season the other side well with salt and pepper. Scatter the anchovies, thyme and extra sage over the livers and cook for 2–3 minutes.

Transfer the liver mixture to a chopping board and use a knife to chop to a rough paste. Return the mixture to the pan over medium heat. Add the saba, cannellini beans, remaining olive oil, and salt and pepper to taste and cook, stirring, for 2–3 minutes.

Finish with a few drops of extra saba and garnish with the fried sage leaves. Serve immediately with the toasted baguette slices.

Pictured page 32.

2 tablespoons extra virgin olive oil

½ brown onion, finely diced

2 cloves garlic, finely chopped

8 Swiss brown mushrooms, diced

1 cup (250 g) risotto rice

sea salt and freshly ground black pepper

1 litre chicken stock

70 g parmesan, finely grated

1 large ball fiore di latte or buffalo mozzarella, diced

2 tablespoons black truffle paste

2 teaspoons truffle oil

vegetable or canola oil, for deep-frying

1½ cups (225 g) plain flour

2 eggs, whisked with 4 tablespoons milk

2 cups (200 g) dried breadcrumbs

lemon wedges, to serve

TRUFFLED MOZZARELLA ARANCINI

These little morsels are addictively delicious. Enjoy them with an aperitif late in the afternoon or as part of an antipasto selection. Here, they are served simply as an appetiser with lemon wedges.

Heat the olive oil in a heavy-based saucepan over medium heat and cook the onion and garlic for about 2 minutes. Add the diced mushroom and rice, season with salt and pepper and stir for 3 minutes. Gradually add the stock, stirring between additions and allowing the liquid to be absorbed before adding more stock – this will take about 15 minutes. When the rice is tender, stir in the parmesan, then spread out on a tray to cool to room temperature. Taste and check the seasoning.

Transfer the cooled risotto to a bowl and combine with the mozzarella, truffle paste and truffle oil. Roll the mixture into walnut-sized balls.

Pour the oil into a heavy-based saucepan to a depth of 4 cm and heat to 180°C or until a cube of bread browns in 15 seconds.

Put the flour, egg mixture and breadcrumbs into three separate shallow dishes. Dip the balls into the flour, then in the egg mixture, then finally into the breadcrumbs and toss gently to coat. You can freeze them at this point, if liked.

Add the balls to the hot oil in batches and cook for 2–4 minutes or until golden. Remove with a slotted spoon and drain on paper towel. Season to taste and serve piping hot with lemon wedges.

Pictured page 33.

Crostini with chicken liver and cannellini
bean pate (see page 30)

Truffled mozzarella arancini (see page 31)

SERVES 4–6

200 ml extra virgin olive oil, plus extra to serve
4 cloves garlic, finely sliced
3 teaspoons fennel seeds, coarsely ground
8 small, ripe tomatoes, sliced into rounds
freshly ground black pepper
1 kg large black mussels, scrubbed and debearded
150 ml red wine
2 large slices sourdough bread, cut in half
1 clove garlic, extra, peeled
fennel fronds, to garnish (optional)

MUSSELS FRIED WITH TOMATO, BLACK PEPPER AND FENNEL SEEDS

This dish is all about the glorious flavour of mussels. It takes just minutes to prepare. Buy the freshest mussels you can for maximum flavour.

Heat the olive oil in a large, deep frying pan over high heat and cook the garlic and fennel seeds for 2 minutes. Add the tomato and lots of black pepper and cook for 1 minute to soften. Add the mussels and wine, then cover the pan with a lid and cook for 2 minutes. Shake the pan and cook for a further 2 minutes. Check that all the shells are open (discard any that are closed or force them open and check them) and remove from the heat.

Meanwhile, toast or grill the bread slices then rub lightly with the garlic clove.

To serve, pile the mussels on the toasted sourdough, pour on the juices and drizzle with a little extra olive oil. Garnish with fennel fronds, if liked.

SERVES 4–6

1 large red onion, sliced

6 free-range chicken leg and thigh portions, halved

1 bulb garlic, squashed

6 slices pancetta

6 sprigs thyme

sea salt and freshly ground black pepper

2 tablespoons extra virgin olive oil

4 tablespoons sherry vinegar

crusty bread, to serve

Parsnip skordalia

3 desiree potatoes, peeled and sliced

3 parsnips, peeled and core removed, cut into 3 cm pieces

3 cloves garlic, peeled

3 tablespoons extra virgin olive oil

150 ml milk

PAN-ROASTED CHICKEN LEGS WITH PARSNIP SKORDALIA

This is a quick and easy dinner for winter, with plenty of vinegary juices just crying out to be mopped up with crusty bread.

Preheat the oven to 200°C (fan-forced).

Arrange the onion over the base of a lightly greased baking dish and top with the chicken pieces. Add the garlic and top with the pancetta and thyme sprigs. Season with salt and pepper and drizzle with the olive oil. Bake for 40 minutes, then remove from the oven and sprinkle with vinegar. Set aside for 5 minutes before serving.

Meanwhile, to make the skordalia, cook the potato, parsnip and garlic in a saucepan of lightly salted boiling water over medium heat for 15–20 minutes or until tender. Drain. Transfer to a food processor, add the olive oil and process for 30 seconds. With the motor running, gradually add the milk and process until the mixture is smooth and creamy. Serve with the chicken pieces and chunks of crusty bread.

SERVES 4–6

1 head spiral broccoli, cut into florets with stems attached
2 bunches broccolini, cut in half on the diagonal
4 tablespoons extra virgin olive oil
5 cloves garlic, sliced
5 anchovies
1 teaspoon dried chilli flakes
60 g butter
4 tablespoons pine nuts, toasted
sea salt and freshly ground black pepper

SPIRAL BROCCOLI WITH BROWN BUTTER, ANCHOVIES AND PINE NUTS

This is delicious with the chicken and skordalia (see previous page) or try it with fish or with crusty bread as a starter. Spiral broccoli is a winter vegetable that is a cross between broccoli and cauliflower. If you can't find it, just use cauliflower or broccoli.

Cook the broccoli and broccolini in a large saucepan of salted boiling water for 4 minutes or until tender. Drain and keep warm.

Heat the olive oil in a large frying pan over high heat and cook the garlic and anchovies for 3 minutes or until the garlic turns golden brown. Add the chilli and butter and allow the mixture to bubble for 1 minute. Add the warm broccoli, broccolini and pine nuts and stir gently to combine. Season with salt and pepper and serve immediately.

SERVES 10

5 eggs, separated

175 g caster sugar

55 g icing sugar

55 g cocoa powder

120 g plain flour

500 ml vanilla ice-cream, softened

200 g orange marmalade

2½ tablespoons water

1 orange, skin and pith removed, segmented

CHOCOLATE ROULADE WITH MARMALADE ICE-CREAM

There is something I love about the combination of ice-cream and frozen cake. It reminds me of the Vienna slices I used to eat as a child. Any leftovers of this delectable dessert may be wrapped loosely in paper and stored in the freezer for 1–2 weeks.

Preheat the oven to 175°C (fan-forced).

Beat the egg yolks and 100 g caster sugar in the bowl of an electric mixer until thick and pale. Whisk the egg whites separately in a clean bowl until soft peaks form, then add the icing sugar and beat until firm.

Sift the cocoa and flour together into a separate bowl. Add half the flour mixture to the egg-yolk mixture and combine well with a metal spoon. Add one quarter of the egg whites to the yolk mixture, then add the remaining flour mixture. Fold in the remaining egg-white mixture.

Line a baking tray with baking paper, leaving a little hanging over the edge. Grease the paper and lightly dust with 1 tablespoon caster sugar. Spread the chocolate mixture over the tray to form a rectangle about 35 cm × 28 cm. Sprinkle with 2 tablespoons caster sugar and bake for 8–12 minutes. Remove from the tray and allow to cool. Peel the paper from the sponge and transfer it to a clean sheet of baking paper that has been lightly dusted with the remaining sugar.

In a bowl, combine the softened ice-cream with half the marmalade and spread the mixture evenly over the sponge. Using the baking paper to help you, carefully roll up the sponge, then wrap it in baking paper and freeze it for 1 hour or until firm. Store for longer if you want to make this ahead of time.

Combine the water and remaining marmalade in a small saucepan over low heat and stir until warmed through and well combined.

To serve, cut the roulade into slices and spoon the marmalade sauce over the top. Scatter with orange segments.

CHEEKY ITALIAN WINTER LUNCH

NORTHERN ITALIAN
OLIVE MILL SOUP

RICOTTA, BABY SPINACH,
WITLOF AND FRESH PEAS

CHOCOLATE MOUSSE AND
HAZELNUT MERINGUE CAKE

SERVES 6

200 g dried borlotti beans, soaked overnight
in hot water
about 3 litres water
2 vegetable stock cubes
1 litre water, extra
3 yellow waxy potatoes, peeled and cut into chunks
120 ml extra virgin olive oil, plus extra to serve
2 brown onions, finely chopped
4 cloves garlic, finely sliced
2 sticks celery, finely chopped
2 carrots, peeled and finely chopped
1 bulb fennel, trimmed and diced
1 tablespoon fennel seeds
2 bay leaves
6 sprigs thyme
400 g can crushed tomatoes
500 g cavolo nero, thick veins removed
250 g white zucchini (courgettes), finely diced
250 g radicchio, coarsely chopped
sea salt and freshly ground black pepper
3 slices ciabatta or sourdough bread
1 clove garlic, extra, peeled
shaved pecorino or parmesan, to serve

NORTHERN ITALIAN OLIVE MILL SOUP

The slow caramelisation of the vegetables gives this robust, peasant-style soup a surprising depth of flavour. It will warm you from top to toe.

Drain the borlotti beans and rinse well. Place the beans in a large saucepan with the water and bring to the boil over high heat, skimming any scum from the surface. Reduce the heat to low and simmer for 1½ hours, adding more water if necessary. By this time the beans will be cooked through and will have absorbed most of the water. Remove half the beans and place in a jug with the stock cubes and extra water and puree with a stick blender until smooth. Add the remaining beans to the jug and set aside.

Place the potato in a medium saucepan of lightly salted water. Bring to the boil over high heat and cook for 15 minutes or until soft and cooked. Drain and set aside.

Meanwhile, heat the olive oil in a large heavy-based saucepan and cook the onion, garlic, celery, carrot and fennel over low heat for 20 minutes or until the vegetables are golden. Stir in the fennel seeds, bay leaves, thyme, crushed tomatoes and pureed bean mixture. Add the cavolo nero, zucchini, radicchio and potato, top up with a little more water and simmer over low heat for 25 minutes until thick and fragrant. Season to taste with salt and pepper.

Toast or grill the bread slices then rub with the garlic clove. Tear into chunks.

Serve the soup with the bread chunks sprinkled over the top. Finish with a scattering of pecorino or parmesan and a generous drizzle of olive oil.

46 CHEEKY ITALIAN WINTER LUNCH

SERVES 6

¾ cup (120 g) fresh peas

2½ tablespoons sherry vinegar

1 red onion, finely sliced

120 ml extra virgin olive oil

sea salt and freshly ground black pepper

3 handfuls baby spinach leaves

2 witlof (chicory), finely sliced

juice of 1 lemon

150 g fresh ricotta, well drained

4 sprigs mint, leaves picked and chopped

lemon wedges, to serve (optional)

RICOTTA, BABY SPINACH, WITLOF AND FRESH PEAS

This salad is delicious and fresh, and goes with just about anything.

Cook the peas in a saucepan of lightly salted boiling water for 4–5 minutes. Drain, refresh under cold water and drain again.

Combine the vinegar, onion and half the olive oil in a bowl. Season with salt and pepper, then add the peas and spinach and toss to coat.

Toss the witlof with the lemon juice and arrange on four serving plates. Top with the peas, then crumble on the ricotta, scatter with the mint and drizzle with the remaining olive oil. Check the seasoning and serve with lemon wedges (if using).

SERVES 6–8

100 ml hazelnut liqueur
cocoa powder, for dusting

Meringue
5 egg whites
225 g caster sugar
150 g ground hazelnuts
115 g butter, melted
70 g plain flour

Chocolate mousse
500 g dark chocolate buttons
4 tablespoons strong coffee
5 egg yolks
600 ml pouring cream, lightly whipped

Toffee
250 g caster sugar
2½ tablespoons water
1 handful hazelnuts, toasted and peeled

CHOCOLATE MOUSSE AND HAZELNUT MERINGUE CAKE

You will need to have quite a few baking trays on hand to bake the five layers of this spectacular meringue cake.

For the meringue, preheat the oven to 130°C (fan-forced). Draw five 20 cm circles on sheets of baking paper, then place the paper on baking trays. Whisk the egg whites in an electric mixer until soft peaks form, then add half the sugar and beat until firm. Using a metal spoon, fold in the remaining sugar and the ground hazelnuts until the sugar has dissolved. Fold in the butter, then sift in the flour and stir to combine. Divide the mixture among the circles on the baking paper and spread thinly with a spatula. Bake in batches for 45 minutes or until light golden. Set aside to cool.

To make the mousse, melt the chocolate in a large heatproof bowl over a saucepan of barely simmering water (don't let the bowl touch the water). Stir in the coffee, then remove the bowl from the heat. Whisk the egg yolks until pale and stir into the chocolate mixture, then stir in the whipped cream. Cover and chill in the fridge for about 10 minutes.

Place a dot of mousse on a platter to anchor the cake. Top with a meringue and sprinkle with liqueur. Spread with some mousse and top with another meringue. Repeat with the remaining mousse and meringue, finishing with a layer of mousse. Chill for 20 minutes.

For the toffee, stir the sugar and water in a saucepan over low heat until the sugar has dissolved. Bring to the boil and cook, without stirring, until the mixture turns a caramel colour. Add the hazelnuts and swirl to coat. Dip the saucepan in a sink of cold water to stop the cooking process. Remove the hazelnuts and set aside. Pour the caramel over a sheet of baking paper to make patterns and allow to set.

When you're ready to serve, decorate the meringue cake with the hazelnuts and toffee and dust with cocoa powder.

Pictured page 42.

LONG LUNCH WITH FRIENDS

BRUSCHETTA WITH SMASHED
BROAD BEANS, GARLIC AND PARMESAN

PAN-FRIED PRAWNS WITH
GREEN CHILLI SAUCE

BAKED POTATOES WITH SOUR CREAM,
HORSERADISH AND BURNT BUTTER

SEARED EYE FILLET WITH PORCINI DRESSING

RHUBARB AND RASPBERRY TARTS

1.6–1.7 kg broad beans

1 clove garlic, peeled

sea salt and freshly ground black pepper

100 ml extra virgin olive oil, plus extra for drizzling

6 thick slices toasted sourdough bread (mixed rye
    or plain flour)

1–2 cloves garlic, extra, peeled

200 g parmesan (preferably parmigiano reggiano),
    shaved

6 slices Spanish jamon or prosciutto

4 sprigs mint, leaves picked and torn

BRUSCHETTA WITH SMASHED BROAD BEANS, GARLIC AND PARMESAN

This dish is all about the combination of flavours –
the sweetness of the smashed broad beans and the
saltiness of the jamon.

Blanch the broad beans in boiling water. Drain, then
double-peel and roughly chop them. You'll need about
2 cups (240 g) all up.

Crush the garlic with a little salt in a large mortar and
pestle. Gradually add the broad beans and olive oil
while pounding until the mixture becomes a green
paste. Season well.

Toast or grill the bread slices then rub with the extra
garlic cloves. Drizzle with a little extra olive oil.

Spread the broad bean mixture over the bread slices
and top with parmesan shavings. Drizzle with extra
olive oil and serve with jamon or prosciutto. Garnish
with fresh mint and a grinding of black pepper.

12 very large raw king prawns

2 tablespoons extra virgin olive oil,
   plus extra for pan-frying

sea salt and freshly ground black pepper

juice of ½ lemon

lemon wedges, to serve (optional)

Green chilli sauce

1 teaspoon black peppercorns

1 teaspoon cumin seeds

1 clove garlic, peeled

2 teaspoons sea salt

3–4 large green chillies, sliced

1 teaspoon diced preserved lemon rind

150 ml extra virgin olive oil

½ bunch coriander, leaves picked

½ bunch flat-leaf parsley, leaves picked

PAN-FRIED PRAWNS WITH GREEN CHILLI SAUCE

This is a great way to cook prawns. Always use large, raw prawns with the shell and head intact, and don't forget to enjoy the sticky richness of the head once cooked – divine! You will need a large heavy-based frying pan (about 36 cm) or two standard frying pans to make this dish.

To make the sauce, grind the peppercorns and cumin seeds to a fine powder in a mortar and pestle. Add the garlic and sea salt and grind for a couple of minutes, then add the chilli, preserved lemon and a little olive oil and grind well. Add the coriander and parsley and gradually drizzle in the remaining olive oil and grind until smooth. Set aside.

Trim the gill-like legs or flippers off the prawns with scissors. Using a small sharp knife, cut through the underside and butterfly the prawns by pressing them flat. Remove the veins. Drizzle with the olive oil and season with salt and pepper.

Heat a little olive oil in a large frying pan over medium heat. Add the prawns, flesh-side down, and cook for 3 minutes. Turn them over and cook the other side briefly until the prawns are just cooked.

Transfer the prawns to a platter, drizzle with lemon juice and spread the green chilli sauce on top. Serve with lemon wedges, if you like.

SERVES 4

500 g rock salt
8 large kipfler potatoes, scrubbed
sea salt and freshly ground black pepper
¾ cup (180 g) sour cream
1 small horseradish root, peeled
    and finely grated
100 g butter
handful watercress leaves

SERVES 4

900 g beef eye fillet, sliced into 4 steaks,
    brought to room temperature
extra virgin olive oil, for drizzling
sea salt and freshly ground black pepper
40 g butter

Porcini dressing
40 g butter
120 ml extra virgin olive oil
400 g Swiss brown mushrooms, diced
1 clove garlic, finely diced
3 golden shallots, finely diced
1 teaspoon dried chilli flakes
sea salt and freshly ground black pepper
3 tablespoons porcini powder

BAKED POTATOES WITH SOUR CREAM, HORSERADISH AND BURNT BUTTER

This is a divine way to serve potatoes and a perfect complement to steak of any type. Cooking the potatoes on rock salt is optional, but it imparts a fantastic pure-potato flavour.

Preheat the oven to 180°C (fan-forced). Spread the rock salt on a baking tray and place the potatoes on the salt. Prick them once with a fork and bake for 40–50 minutes until tender.

Remove the potatoes from the oven and place them on a plate. Split them lengthways, pushing them open a little with your fingers. Season with a little salt and pepper, then spoon some sour cream onto each potato and grate over the horseradish.

Cook the butter in a small saucepan over high heat for 2 minutes until nut brown. Pour the butter over the potatoes, followed by a scattering of watercress. Serve with the eye fillet.

SEARED EYE FILLET WITH PORCINI DRESSING >

The porcini mushroom dressing adds a deliciously earthy taste to simply seared steak.

To make the dressing, heat the butter and 1 tablespoon of the oil in a large frying pan over high heat. Cook the diced mushroom for 4 minutes, then add the garlic and shallot and cook for a further 2 minutes. Remove from the heat, sprinkle over the chilli and season with salt and pepper. Stir in the porcini powder and remaining oil.

Put the steaks on a plate, drizzle lightly with oil and season with salt and pepper.

Heat a large heavy-based frying pan over high heat. Cook the steaks for 3 minutes on one side, then turn them over, add the butter and cook for a further 2 minutes. Remove the steaks from the pan and rest for 2 minutes on a warm plate.

Cut the steaks in half through the middle and place on a hot platter or individual dinner plates. Spoon over the porcini dressing and serve with the baked potatoes.

MAKES ABOUT 24

200 ml pouring cream, whipped
icing sugar, for dusting

Pastry
75 g caster sugar
180 g butter
2 egg yolks
1 tablespoon water
250 g plain flour, sifted

Rhubarb and raspberry filling
8 sticks rhubarb, trimmed and
  sliced into 2 cm pieces
1 cup (220 g) raw sugar
2½ tablespoons orange juice
2 × 150 g punnets raspberries

RHUBARB AND RASPBERRY TARTS

These little tarts have just enough sweetness, creaminess and tartness to showcase the fruit and pastry. Great for afternoon tea or as a cheeky dessert.

To make the pastry, briefly process the sugar and butter in a food processor. Add the egg yolks and water and process until just combined, then add the flour and process until the mixture just comes together. Tip out the pastry onto a floured work surface and gently press it into a ball. Wrap the pastry in plastic film and place in the fridge for 30 minutes.

Divide the pastry into two portions. Roll out one portion between two sheets of baking paper to a thickness of about 4 mm and cut out rounds using a 6 cm cutter. Place the pastry in 5 cm round tartlet moulds. Repeat with the remaining pastry, then refrigerate for 15 minutes.

Preheat the oven to 180°C (fan-forced).

Line the pastry cases with baking paper and fill with pastry weights or uncooked rice. Bake for 5 minutes, then remove the weights and bake for a further 4–5 minutes or until golden and cooked. Remove the baking paper and weights and leave to cool.

To make the filling, combine the rhubarb, sugar and orange juice in a saucepan. Stir and set aside for 15 minutes, then cook over medium heat for about 4–5 minutes or until the rhubarb is just tender. Stir in the raspberries, then remove the pan from the heat and leave to cool to room temperature.

To serve, spoon the rhubarb filling into the tart cases and serve topped with a dollop of cream and a light dusting of icing sugar.

SUMMER FEAST

POTATO FOCACCIA WITH ANCHOVIES AND CARAMELISED ONION

CALAMARI SEARED WITH POTATO, RADICCHIO AND FRIED BREADCRUMBS

CHARGRILLED SCOTCH FILLET WITH SUMMER HERBED OIL, RICOTTA AND LEMON

RICOTTA SALATA WITH TOMATOES, ONION AND BASIL

CHERRY AND ALMOND BURNT-BUTTER TORTE

500 g potatoes, peeled and cut into
   similar-sized chunks

1 kg plain flour

1 tablespoon sea salt

2½ teaspoons dried yeast

775 ml warm water

3½ tablespoons extra virgin olive oil

4 large red onions, thinly sliced

6 cloves garlic, thinly sliced

sea salt and freshly ground black pepper

10 anchovies, halved lengthways

½ bunch oregano, leaves picked

POTATO FOCACCIA WITH ANCHOVIES AND CARAMELISED ONION

This light and fluffy focaccia is delicious served on its own or as part of a shared table or antipasto platter. The onions and anchovies inside the bread add a delicious sweet and salty flavour combination.

Cook the potato in lightly salted boiling water until tender. Drain. Press the potato through a mouli or potato ricer into the bowl of an electric mixer (you will need a dough hook attachment). Add the flour and salt and mix lightly with your hands. Whisk the yeast into the water and add to the potato. Mix on low speed to combine, then increase the speed to high until the dough is sticky (this should take about 9 minutes). Cover the bowl with plastic film and set aside in a warm place for 30 minutes or until the dough has doubled in size.

Meanwhile, heat 2½ tablespoons olive oil in a frying pan over medium heat. Add the onion and garlic and cook for 20–30 minutes or until caramelised. Season and set aside.

Preheat the oven to 220°C (fan-forced). Line a large baking tray with baking paper (I use a 40 cm round iron tray) or use two smaller ones. Press half the dough onto the tray until it reaches the edge, then drizzle with olive oil and cover with plastic film. Put the tray in a warm place for 15 minutes or until the dough has risen. Leave the remaining dough in the bowl, cover and set aside for 15 minutes until risen.

Remove the plastic film from the tray and spread the caramelised onion, anchovies and oregano over the dough. Stretch the remaining dough and drape over the top as best you can – it will not be perfect. Season with salt and pepper and bake for 30–45 minutes or until golden. If you like it really crunchy, let it sit for 5 minutes then slide the focaccia out of the tray onto a cooling rack that can go in the oven and cook for another 10 minutes or so. Allow to cool to warm room temperature before cutting.

Calamari seared with potato, radicchio and fried breadcrumbs (see page 66)

2 large potatoes, peeled and cut into chunks

3 thick slices sourdough bread

1 clove garlic, peeled

2 handfuls flat-leaf parsley leaves

150 ml extra virgin olive oil

4 calamari hoods, cleaned, with wings attached
    and legs trimmed

sea salt and freshly ground black pepper

3 cloves garlic, extra, finely chopped

1 teaspoon dried chilli flakes

1 small head radicchio, torn into bite-sized pieces

juice of 1 large lemon

1 bulb fennel, trimmed and cut into thin wedges

CALAMARI SEARED WITH POTATO, RADICCHIO AND FRIED BREADCRUMBS

This rustic dish is a great way to enjoy calamari, covered in garlicky crumbs, bitter leaves, fennel and freshly squeezed lemon juice.

Cook the potato in a saucepan of lightly salted boiling water until tender. Drain, then break up with a fork.

Toast or grill the bread slices, then rub well with the garlic clove. Tear into chunks and place in a food processor with half the parsley and process to coarse breadcrumbs.

Heat 2½ tablespoons olive oil in a frying pan over medium heat and add the breadcrumb mixture. Toss for 3–4 minutes or until golden, then set aside to cool.

Cut the calamari into 2 cm rings and the legs into three pieces. Toss with 1 tablespoon olive oil and season with salt and pepper.

Heat 2 tablespoons olive oil in a very large frying pan over high heat and cook the calamari for 1–2 minutes. Add the garlic and chilli and cook for 1 minute. Stir and cook for another 2 minutes, then add the warm potato, radicchio, lemon juice, fennel, remaining parsley and half the breadcrumbs. Stir again, then serve scattered with the remaining breadcrumbs and drizzled with the remaining olive oil.

¼ bunch chives, snipped

¼ bunch tarragon, chopped

6 sprigs flat-leaf parsley, chopped

¼ bunch chervil, chopped

2 cloves garlic, finely sliced

1 teaspoon dried chilli flakes

120 ml extra virgin olive oil, plus extra to serve

finely grated zest of 1 lemon

salt flakes and freshly ground black pepper

2 × 450 g scotch fillet steaks at room temperature,
   both sides brushed with a little olive oil

150 g fresh ricotta, well drained

1 lemon, cut into wedges

10–12 radishes, cleaned (with leaves if possible)

100 ml extra virgin olive oil

45 ml sherry vinegar

1 clove garlic, finely chopped

1 teaspoon sugar

sea salt and freshly ground black pepper

850 g tomatoes (use a mix, including cherry and grape)

½ bunch basil, leaves picked

1 red onion, halved and thinly sliced

100 g ricotta salata, shaved

< CHARGRILLED SCOTCH FILLET WITH SUMMER HERBED OIL, RICOTTA AND LEMON

This takes no time at all to cook, and I love the zing from the lemon and chilli – it's the perfect way to enjoy steak through the hotter months of the year. Make sure the steaks are at room temperature before cooking.

Combine the chives, tarragon, parsley and chervil in a bowl. Whisk together the garlic, chilli flakes, olive oil and lemon zest in a small bowl and pour over the herbs. Season with salt and pepper.

Preheat a chargrill or barbecue plate to hot (smoking) and sear the steaks for 5 minutes. Turn and cook for another 5 minutes, then transfer to a chopping board and rest for 5 minutes.

Cut the steak into thick slices and arrange on serving plates. Dollop with ricotta and spoon over the herbed oil, then drizzle with extra olive oil and a squeeze of lemon juice. Serve immediately, scattered with the radishes.

RICOTTA SALATA WITH TOMATOES, ONION AND BASIL

Ricotta salata is salted, dried sheep or buffalo ricotta curd. It has a nutty flavour and can be used in place of parmesan. Look for it at your local deli or speciality cheese supplier. To get the most out of this salad you will need fragrant, sun-kissed tomatoes – it really doesn't matter what sort, just as long as they taste wonderful.

Make a dressing by mixing together the olive oil, vinegar, garlic, sugar, salt and pepper in a small bowl.

Slice, quarter or leave the tomatoes whole, depending on size. Place the tomatoes, basil and onion in a serving bowl and gently toss together. Add the dressing and toss again. Top with shaved ricotta salata.

Pictured page 60.

SERVES 8

cooking spray

180 g butter

1½ vanilla beans, split, seeds scraped
    and cut into fine splinters

5 egg whites, at room temperature

pinch of salt

340 g icing sugar, sifted, plus extra for dusting

110 g plain flour

100 g ground almonds

½ teaspoon almond essence

2 tablespoons flaked or slivered almonds

300 g cherries, pitted and halved

creme fraiche, to serve

CHERRY AND ALMOND BURNT-BUTTER TORTE

This tart is a complete delight to eat and is easy to make as there is no fiddly pastry. You could replace the cherries with fresh raspberries or blackberries or even ripe figs, or use a combination of fruit.

Preheat the oven to 160°C (fan-forced). Line a 24 cm × 5 cm fluted loose-based tin with baking paper and spray with cooking spray.

Melt the butter in a small saucepan. Add the vanilla beans and seeds and cook over medium heat for 4–5 minutes or until the mixture darkens and develops a nutty aroma. Pour into a bowl and cool to room temperature. Remove some of the vanilla splinters and set aside for garnish.

Place the egg whites and a pinch of salt in a large clean bowl and whisk until soft peaks form. Add half the icing sugar and combine, then fold in the remaining icing sugar, flour and ground almonds. Stir in the burnt vanilla butter and almond essence.

Pour the mixture into the tin and scatter over the almonds and cherries (reserving a few for garnish). Bake for 1 hour or until the torte is puffed and just set. Remove from the oven and cool to room temperature.

Dust with icing sugar and garnish with the reserved cherries and vanilla-bean splinters. Serve with a generous spoonful of creme fraiche.

EARLY SPRING
EXTRAVAGANZA

FLATHEAD AND POTATO FISHCAKES

BAGNA CAUDA WITH SOFT-BOILED EGGS
AND ASPARAGUS

BLUE EYE WITH FRIED BUTTER BEANS AND
GARLIC AND SOUR LEMON DRESSING

ROAST RACK OF LAMB WITH CAPSICUM, TOMATOES
ON THE VINE AND SMASHED BROAD BEANS

CAMPARI AND BLOOD ORANGE JELLIES
WITH VANILLA ICE-CREAM

4 flathead fillets (about 350 g in total)

1 cup (300 g) rock salt, crushed

500 g waxy yellow potatoes, peeled

4 sprigs oregano, leaves picked and chopped

8 sprigs flat-leaf parsley, leaves picked and chopped

finely grated zest of ½ lemon

1½ cloves garlic, peeled

sea salt and freshly ground black pepper

300 ml milk

1 teaspoon black peppercorns

2 bay leaves

3 eggs, separated

½ cup (75 g) plain flour

1 cup (70 g) Japanese panko breadcrumbs

vegetable oil, for pan-frying

lemon slices, to serve

whole-egg mayonnaise, to serve

FLATHEAD AND POTATO FISHCAKES

These superb tapas-style fishcakes are delicious either on their own or with a salad. I like to use Japanese panko breadcrumbs because they give a lighter, crisper coating than regular breadcrumbs. They're readily available from Asian food stores and some larger supermarkets.

Place the fish fillets on a plate, cover with rock salt and set aside for 1 hour. This lightly cures the fish, giving a wonderful flavour and texture.

Cook the potatoes in salted boiling water for about 15–20 minutes or until tender. Drain, then mash while still hot.

Place the oregano, parsley, lemon zest, ½ clove garlic and a pinch of salt in a mortar and pestle and pound to a paste. Set aside.

Shake the excess rock salt from the fish. Combine the milk, peppercorns, bay leaves and remaining garlic in a medium saucepan and bring to the boil over high heat. Reduce the heat to low, add the fish and simmer gently for 5 minutes. Remove the pan from the heat and set aside for 3 minutes, then remove the fish with a slotted spoon and place on a plate. Cool slightly.

Flake the fish into a bowl and mix with the oregano paste. Stir in the potato and fold in the egg yolks. Season with pepper and refrigerate for 15 minutes.

Mould the fish mixture into torpedo shapes about 5 cm long. Whisk the egg whites in a bowl to break them up. Place the flour and breadcrumbs in separate shallow bowls. Dust the fishcakes lightly with flour, then dip them in the egg white and coat with the breadcrumbs, shaking off any excess.

Pour the vegetable oil into a deep heavy-based frying pan to a depth of 5 cm and heat over medium heat. Add the fishcakes (in batches if necessary – you don't want to crowd the pan) and cook for 3–4 minutes or until golden. Drain on paper towel.

Serve the fishcakes with lemon slices and a dollop of mayonnaise.

2 large eggs

2 bunches asparagus, trimmed

8 zucchini (courgette) flowers or 8 small zucchini
   (courgettes), cut in half

2 tablespoons extra virgin olive oil

sea salt and freshly ground black pepper

60 g grana padano, shaved (optional)

Bagna cauda

3 tablespoons extra virgin olive oil

60 g butter

7 anchovies, chopped

1 clove garlic, finely diced

1 teaspoon freshly ground black pepper

1 tablespoon warm water

BAGNA CAUDA WITH SOFT-BOILED EGGS AND ASPARAGUS

Bagna cauda is warm olive oil infused with anchovies,
butter and garlic – it's heavenly. Try it also with
steamed vegetables, fish or crusty bread.

To make the bagna cauda, heat the olive oil, butter,
anchovies, garlic and pepper in a small saucepan over
low heat until warm. Stir in the water and set aside.

Bring a small saucepan of water to the boil over high
heat, add the eggs and cook for 6 minutes. When the
eggs are cool enough to handle, peel them and set aside.

Bring a saucepan of lightly salted water to the boil over
high heat. Add the asparagus and cook for 3 minutes.
Halfway through the cooking time, add the zucchini.
Drain, then toss in the olive oil and season to taste.

Place the asparagus and zucchini on a platter. Slice the
eggs in half and arrange them on top, then sprinkle
with the grana padano shavings (if using). Spoon over
the warm dressing and serve.

Pictured page 75.

850 g blue-eye fillet, skin on, all bones removed

2 tablespoons extra virgin olive oil

sea salt

400 g can butter beans, drained and rinsed,
    then drizzled with a little olive oil

Garlic and sour lemon dressing

4 tablespoons extra virgin olive oil

4 cloves garlic, thinly sliced

1 teaspoon fennel seeds, toasted and coarsely ground

1 celery heart, finely sliced and baby leaves reserved

sea salt and freshly ground black pepper

1 tablespoon finely chopped preserved lemon rind

2 lemons, skin and pith removed, segmented and
    cut into triangles

1 small red chilli, finely sliced

1 green chilli, seeds removed, finely sliced

6 sprigs coriander, leaves picked and chopped

2 sprigs tarragon, leaves picked

4 sprigs flat-leaf parsley, leaves picked and chopped

BLUE EYE WITH FRIED BUTTER BEANS AND GARLIC AND SOUR LEMON DRESSING

It is well worth putting in the effort to make this dish. The fried butter beans are a complete delight, and the garlic dressing, spiked with chilli, lemon and parsley, has a refreshing kick that goes beautifully with the pan-fried fish.

Preheat the oven to 180°C (fan-forced).

Use a sharp knife to score the skin side of the fish fillet lengthways, then drizzle with the olive oil and season with salt.

To make the dressing, place the olive oil and garlic in a medium frying pan over medium heat and cook for a few minutes until the garlic starts to colour. Add the fennel seeds and celery, then season with salt and pepper. Stir for 20 seconds, then remove from the heat. Tip into a bowl and allow to cool slightly, then add the remaining ingredients. Stir well, then taste and adjust the seasoning if necessary.

Heat a large non-stick frying pan with an ovenproof handle over high heat for 2 minutes. Add the fish, skin-side down, and cook for 6 minutes. Transfer the pan to the oven and bake for 8 minutes, then remove and allow to rest for 4 minutes. (If you don't have an ovenproof frying pan, transfer the fish to a baking tray and cook for an additional 4 minutes.) Lift out the fish and place on a platter. In the same pan, cook the butter beans over high heat for 2–3 minutes or until the skin scorches and curls.

Arrange the butter beans on and around the fish, drizzle with the dressing and scatter with the reserved celery leaves. Serve immediately.

Pictured page 72.

2 red capsicums (peppers)

2 × 9-point lamb racks with a cap of fat left on
  (ask your butcher), at room temperature

3 handfuls small tomatoes on the vine

extra virgin olive oil, for drizzling

100 g feta

Oregano marinade

1 tablespoon dried oregano

2 cloves garlic, finely chopped

2½ tablespoons olive oil

sea salt and freshly ground black pepper

Smashed broad beans

2 cups (350 g) broad beans

1 cup (120 g) frozen peas

6 sprigs mint, leaves picked and coarsely chopped

½ clove garlic, peeled

sea salt

100 ml extra virgin olive oil

ROAST RACK OF LAMB WITH CAPSICUM, TOMATOES ON THE VINE AND SMASHED BROAD BEANS

Buy a couple of racks of lamb for this and cut them into cutlets yourself – the smaller ones are sweeter and juicier.

Preheat the oven to 180°C (fan-forced). Place the whole capsicums in the oven and roast for 30 minutes until blistered. Cover with a tea towel and leave to cool, then slip off the skins and tear each capsicum into four pieces.

Score the top of the lamb racks in a criss-cross pattern. This allows the fat to render during cooking and helps the marinade to penetrate.

To make the oregano marinade, combine all the ingredients in a small bowl. Spread the paste over the lamb racks and set aside.

To make the smashed broad beans, cook the broad beans in lightly salted boiling water for 2–3 minutes, then drain and refresh under cold water. Blanch the peas in lightly salted boiling water for 1 minute, then drain.

Remove the outer shell from the broad beans and coarsely chop the beans. Place half the beans in a mortar and pestle, add the mint, garlic and salt to taste and pound to a rough paste. Add the peas, olive oil and remaining beans and pound to the consistency of mashed potato.

Heat a large non-stick frying pan over high heat, add the lamb racks, skin-side down and cook for 6 minutes each side. Transfer to a baking tray, arrange the vine tomatoes and capsicum around the lamb (making sure it is a snug fit) and drizzle with olive oil. Place in the oven and roast for about 10–12 minutes or until cooked to your liking. Remove and rest the lamb for 5 minutes.

Cut the lamb into double cutlets and divide among plates with the broad bean paste. Serve with the capsicum, tomatoes and a scattering of feta.

SERVES 4–6

8 leaves gold-strength gelatine

450 ml freshly squeezed blood orange juice, strained

185 g caster sugar, plus extra for dusting

120 ml Campari

1 ruby grapefruit or blood orange, skin and pith removed,
    segmented and drained on paper towel

vanilla ice-cream, to serve

icing sugar, for dusting

Persian fairy floss, to serve (optional)

CAMPARI AND BLOOD ORANGE JELLIES WITH VANILLA ICE-CREAM

The combination of bitter Campari and blood orange juice makes a drink that's so delicious and refreshing that I decided to turn it into a jelly. It's particularly good after a rich main course: jelly and ice-cream – what's not to like? Gold-strength gelatine leaves are available from delis and specialist food stores.

Soak the gelatine leaves in cold water until soft, then squeeze to remove any excess water.

Place the blood orange juice in a small saucepan over low heat and bring to a simmer. Skim the surface, then add the sugar and stir until dissolved. Remove from the heat and pour half of the liquid into a bowl. Add the softened gelatine to the remaining juice, stir until smooth and set aside to cool. Strain the mixture, then stir in the Campari and remaining juice.

Pour the mixture into chilled glasses. Cover and refrigerate for 3 hours or until set.

When you're nearly ready to serve, dust the grapefruit or orange segments in caster sugar. Roll small scoops of ice-cream in icing sugar. Arrange the fruit segments over the jellies, top with a scoop of ice-cream and finish with Persian fairy floss (if using).

HIGH TEA

SOUR CHERRY AND RICOTTA STRUDEL

CROSTOLI KNOTS WITH HONEY,
ORANGE BLOSSOM AND SESAME

HOKEY POKEY ROCKY ROAD

COCONUT BUTTER CAKE WITH
PASSIONFRUIT ICING

LAYERED CREPE CAKE WITH WALNUT
JAM AND CHOCOLATE GANACHE

STICKY GINGER AND PEAR CAKE

RASPBERRY-ICED CUPCAKES

SERVES 4

375 g filo pastry

210 g butter, melted

650 g jar sour cherries, drained, syrup reserved

1 punnet (150 g) raspberries

4 tablespoons Japanese panko breadcrumbs
  (or use fresh breadcrumbs)

1 tablespoon caster sugar

1 vanilla bean, cut into thin strips

100 g raspberry jam

Ricotta filling

350 g fresh ricotta, well drained

1 large egg

2 large egg yolks

150 g caster sugar

finely grated zest and juice of 1 lemon

2 teaspoons vanilla extract

SOUR CHERRY AND RICOTTA STRUDEL

I always loved strudel as a child and this one, with its blend of sour cherries and ricotta, is truly magnificent.

Preheat the oven to 180°C (fan-forced). Line a 50 cm × 30 cm baking tray with baking paper.

To make the ricotta filling, combine all the ingredients in a bowl.

Brush one sheet of filo pastry with melted butter. Place another sheet on top, slightly to one side, to form a rectangle about 45 cm long. Repeat layering and buttering until all the pastry has been used (reserve the rest of the butter for later). Spread the ricotta mixture over the pastry, leaving a 5 cm border. Sprinkle the cherries, raspberries and breadcrumbs over the top.

Roll up the strudel from a narrow end, tucking in the edges as you go to prevent the filling leaking. Place the strudel on the prepared tray, seam-side down, and use a sharp knife to diagonally score the top. Brush with the remaining melted butter and sprinkle with the caster sugar and vanilla bean strips. Bake for 55 minutes, then remove from the oven and set aside for 25 minutes before serving.

Place the raspberry jam and reserved cherry syrup in a small saucepan and bring to the boil over medium heat. Reduce the heat and simmer for 15 minutes or until the liquid has reduced by a third. Set aside to cool.

Cut the strudel into slices with a serrated knife and serve with the sauce.

3 small eggs

130 g icing sugar, plus extra for dusting

470 g plain flour

1 teaspoon vanilla extract

75 ml Marsala

vegetable oil, for deep-frying

3 tablespoons orange blossom water

½ cup (175 g) honey

100 g sesame seeds

250 g dark chocolate, broken into small pieces

250 g milk chocolate, broken into small pieces

120 g vanilla marshmallows, halved

40 g shaved coconut

140 g rose Turkish delight, cut into 2 cm pieces

45 g glace cherries

90 g almonds, toasted and chopped

40 g unsalted pistachio kernels

40 g craisins

CROSTOLI KNOTS WITH HONEY, ORANGE BLOSSOM AND SESAME

This Italian recipe has a lovely Middle Eastern twist with the addition of sesame seeds, honey and orange blossom water. It is always a favourite at our family get-togethers.

Using an electric mixer, beat the eggs and icing sugar until thick and frothy. Change to a dough hook, add the flour, vanilla and Marsala and knead the mix for about 10 minutes until smooth and elastic. Remove and rest for 5 minutes.

Turn out the dough onto a lightly floured surface and cut it into four pieces. Roll each portion into a 20 cm × 12 cm rectangle. Using a crinkle wheel-cutter, cut strips of dough about 3.5 cm wide and tie in a loose knot. Place on a floured tray.

Heat the vegetable oil in a large heavy-based saucepan or deep-fryer to 180°C or until a cube of bread browns in 15 seconds. Add the crostoli in batches and cook for 2–3 minutes or until golden and cooked through. Drain on a wire rack. Sprinkle with orange blossom water while still hot, then drizzle with honey and sprinkle with sesame seeds. Dust with extra icing sugar. Crostoli will keep in an airtight container for up to 2 days.

HOKEY POKEY ROCKY ROAD

When I make rocky road, I include every single ingredient that I love personally. The combination of dark and milk chocolate makes this one extra special.

Line a shallow 30 cm × 10 cm loaf tin with baking paper.

Melt the dark and milk chocolate in a large heatproof bowl over a saucepan of barely simmering water (don't let the bowl touch the water).

Combine the remaining ingredients in a separate bowl. Pour on the melted chocolate and use a large spoon to fold it through. Stand for 5 minutes, then pour the mixture into the prepared tin and refrigerate for about 30 minutes or until set. Cut into large chunks before serving.

Crostoli knots with honey, orange blossom
and sesame (see page 88)

Sour cherry and strudel (see page 84)

SERVES 8–10

125 ml milk

80 g plain yoghurt

1½ teaspoons vanilla extract

250 g plain flour

1½ teaspoons baking powder

½ teaspoon bicarbonate of soda

¼ teaspoon salt

120 g desiccated coconut

130 g unsalted butter

200 g caster sugar

3 large eggs

Passionfruit icing

300 g unsalted butter, at room temperature

700 g icing sugar, sifted

pulp of 6 passionfruit

pulp of 4 passionfruit, extra, to decorate

COCONUT BUTTER CAKE WITH PASSIONFRUIT ICING

A little coconut sprinkled here and there can instantly change and define a recipe. Here it adds a delicious density to the cake, and a generous coating of passionfruit icing makes it irresistible.

Preheat the oven to 160°C (fan-forced) and line a 25 cm round cake tin with baking paper.

Combine the milk, yoghurt and vanilla in a bowl.

Sift the flour, baking powder, bicarbonate of soda and salt into a bowl, then stir in the coconut.

Beat the butter and sugar with a whisk until pale and fluffy. Add the eggs one at a time, beating well between additions, then alternately add the milk mixture and dry ingredients, blending well between additions. Pour the batter into the cake tin and bake for 40 minutes or until a skewer inserted into the centre comes out clean. Cool in the tin for 20 minutes before turning out onto a serving plate.

To make the icing, beat the butter really well in an electric mixer, then add the icing sugar and the passionfruit pulp.

Split the cake in two horizontally and sandwich together with half the icing. Spoon the remaining icing over the top and smooth the surface. Spoon over the extra pulp and set aside for 30 minutes before serving.

SERVES 6–10

4 eggs, beaten

420 ml milk

250 g pouring cream

125 g butter, melted

1 teaspoon vanilla extract

300 g plain flour

1 teaspoon baking powder

2 tablespoons icing sugar, sifted

butter, extra, for pan-frying

Walnut jam

375 g walnuts, lightly toasted and cooled

350 ml pouring cream

165 g icing sugar

80 ml strong espresso

2 teaspoons ground cinnamon

Chocolate ganache

150 g dark chocolate, broken into pieces

¼ teaspoon cornflour

170 g pouring cream, at room temperature

30 g butter

LAYERED CREPE CAKE WITH WALNUT JAM AND CHOCOLATE GANACHE

This cake is divinely rich and so decadent that I can usually only manage a small slice. The crepe mix can be made a day ahead if you want, but the walnut jam and assembled cake should be made on the day – do not refrigerate.

Whisk together the eggs, milk, cream, butter and vanilla in a bowl.

Sift the flour, baking powder and icing sugar into a separate bowl and make a well in the middle. Pour in the milk mixture and whisk to make a batter.

Melt a little butter in a non-stick frying pan over medium heat. Pour in enough batter to make a 25 cm crepe and cook until lightly golden on both sides. Remove and keep warm. Repeat with the remaining mixture to make 15 crepes, adding more butter as needed.

To make the walnut jam, place the walnuts in a food processor and grind to a fine powder. Place in a medium heavy-based saucepan, add the remaining ingredients and stir over medium heat for 15–20 minutes until thickened. Spoon into a clean bowl and allow to cool to room temperature.

To make the ganache, melt the chocolate in a large heatproof bowl over a saucepan of barely simmering water (don't let the bowl touch the water). Mix the cornflour into the cream. Add the butter and cream mixture to the chocolate and stir until thick and smooth.

To assemble the cake, place a crepe on a serving plate and spread evenly with the walnut jam. Repeat with the remaining crepes and jam, finishing with a crepe. Pour the ganache over the top and set aside for 10 minutes. Cut into wedges to serve.

220 g golden syrup

170 g sour cream

100 g brown sugar

2 eggs

280 g butter, melted

2 teaspoons grated ginger

finely grated zest of ½ lemon

90 g plain flour

130 g self-raising flour

40 g semolina

2 teaspoons ground ginger

½ teaspoon salt

1 teaspoon baking powder

pouring cream, to serve (optional)

Topping

80 g butter

110 g brown sugar

½ teaspoon salt

125 g glace ginger, sliced

2 pears, peeled and finely sliced

STICKY GINGER AND PEAR CAKE

This cake is sticky, golden and delicious, with a great buttery taste.

Preheat the oven to 180°C (fan-forced). Line the base of a 24 cm springform tin with baking paper.

To make the topping, melt the butter in a small saucepan over low heat. Stir in the brown sugar and salt until combined, then pour the mixture into the tin and spread evenly over the base. Arrange the ginger and pear pieces decoratively over the top.

Whisk together the golden syrup, sour cream, brown sugar and eggs. Add the melted butter and whisk to combine, then stir in the grated ginger and lemon zest.

Sift the flours, semolina, ground ginger, salt and baking powder into a separate bowl, then fold in the golden syrup mixture.

Carefully pour the cake batter into the tin, over the topping, and gently tap the tin to remove any air bubbles. Bake for 50 minutes or until a skewer comes out clean. Remove from the oven and allow the cake to cool in the tin on a wire rack. To serve, invert the cake onto a platter and serve with cream, if desired.

MAKES 18

250 g unsalted butter, softened

200 g caster sugar

4 eggs

250 g self-raising flour

2 teaspoons baking powder

1 teaspoon vanilla extract

100 ml milk

1 large punnet (about 250 g) raspberries

160 g icing sugar, sifted

RASPBERRY-ICED CUPCAKES

Who doesn't love cupcakes? The berry icing makes these ones look and taste divine.

Preheat the oven to 180°C (fan-forced). Line 18 regular muffin holes with paper patty pans.

Place the butter, sugar, eggs, flour, baking powder and vanilla extract in a food processor and process until smooth. Gradually add the milk until the mixture is smooth and combined.

Spoon the batter into the muffin holes until each patty pan is two-thirds full. Bake for 15–20 minutes or until a skewer inserted into the centre comes out clean. Remove from the tin and cool on wire racks.

Take out 18 perfect raspberries and set aside for garnish. Place the icing sugar and remaining raspberries in a food processor and blend well. Spread the icing over the cooled cupcakes and decorate with reserved raspberries.

SIMPLE SUNDAY

ROAST CHICKEN STUFFED WITH PARSLEY,
HAZELNUTS AND BUTTER

SIMPLE POTATO DAUPHINOISE

CREAMED SPINACH

CHOCOLATE AND ORANGE CREME CARAMEL

2 red onions, thickly sliced

1 tablespoon sea salt, or to taste

4 cloves garlic, sliced

½ teaspoon black peppercorns

1 tablespoon olive oil

½ bunch flat-leaf parsley, leaves picked and chopped

50 g hazelnuts, toasted and coarsely chopped

100 g butter, softened

1.6 kg free-range chicken

sea salt and freshly ground black pepper

1 lemon, sliced

ROAST CHICKEN STUFFED WITH PARSLEY, HAZELNUTS AND BUTTER

Placing herbs and nuts under the chicken's skin gives this dish its wonderful flavour and crispy texture.

Preheat the oven to 200°C (fan-forced). Line a baking dish or cast-iron dish with onion slices (the dish should be just large enough to hold the chicken).

Gently pound the salt, garlic, peppercorns and olive oil in a mortar and pestle. Gradually add the parsley and hazelnuts and pound to a rough paste. Spoon the mixture into a bowl and stir in the butter.

Dry the chicken inside and out with paper towel and season well. Make small pockets under the breast and leg skin using your fingers, then gently spread the stuffing over the breast and legs between the skin and meat (take care not to tear the skin). Stuff lemon slices into the cavity and place the chicken on the onions in the baking dish.

Roast for about 1¼ hours, basting with the pan juices halfway through the cooking time. The chicken should be golden and cooked through. Check by inserting a skewer in the thickest part of the thigh – if the juices are still a bit pink, roast for another 10 minutes or so. Rest for 10 minutes before serving.

Pictured page 108.

SERVES 4–6

1 large clove garlic, peeled and cut in half
5 sprigs thyme, leaves picked
220 ml thickened cream
2 tablespoons sour cream
300 ml chicken stock
100 g butter
sea salt and freshly ground black pepper
8 dutch potatoes, peeled

SERVES 4

2½ tablespoons olive oil
2 cloves garlic, finely chopped
3 golden shallots, finely chopped
6 sprigs flat-leaf parsley, leaves picked
   and finely chopped
6 basil leaves, torn
600 g baby spinach, washed and drained
sea salt and freshly ground black pepper
50 g butter
150 ml pouring cream
ground nutmeg, to taste

SIMPLE POTATO DAUPHINOISE

Rich and buttery, this luscious side dish is perfect
served with braised or roast meat, or you can serve it
as a light meal with a green salad.

Preheat the oven to 200°C (fan-forced). Rub the
bottom of a heavy, round 25 cm × 8 cm ovenproof
dish with half a garlic clove.

Place the garlic halves, thyme, cream, sour cream, stock
and butter in a saucepan over low heat until warm.
Remove from the heat and season with salt and pepper.

Use a mandolin or a sharp knife to cut the potatoes
into 2.5 mm thick slices.

Just before cooking, ladle 125 ml of the cream mixture
into the dish, followed by an overlapping layer of
potatoes. Season lightly, then continue layering with
the remaining cream and potato slices. Pour the last of
the cream mixture over the top. Cover with a sheet
of baking paper, then a sheet of foil and seal tightly.

Place on a tray (to catch any mess) and bake on the
bottom shelf of the oven for 1 hour, then remove the
paper and foil and bake for a further 15 minutes or
until puffed and golden. Remove from the oven and
allow to stand for 5 minutes before serving.

Pictured page 109.

CREAMED SPINACH

This is the ultimate accompaniment to steak or fish.
It is decadently rich but if you can forgive the cream
and butter, it's good for you too.

Heat the olive oil in a very large, deep frying pan over
medium heat and cook the garlic and shallot for about
2–3 minutes. Add the parsley, basil and spinach, season
to taste and cook over high heat for 2–3 minutes. Add
the butter, cream and nutmeg and cook for a further
3–4 minutes. Remove a third of the spinach and puree
the remaining mixture with a stick blender. Return the
whole spinach to the pan and stir well.

Pictured page 104.

Roast chicken stuffed with parsley, hazelnuts and butter (see page 106)

Simple potato dauphinoise (see page 107)

finely grated zest of 2 oranges

160 g dark chocolate buttons

600 ml milk

250 g caster sugar, plus 3 tablespoons extra

120 ml water

4 large eggs

2 egg yolks

CHOCOLATE AND ORANGE CREME CARAMEL

I love this dessert. It has a delicious combination of flavours and textures – the orange in the custard and the richness of the chocolate and caramel create a rich treat.

Preheat the oven to 160°C (fan-forced).

Combine the orange zest and chocolate buttons in a small bowl. Bring the milk to a simmer in a small saucepan and pour over the chocolate. Stir until the chocolate has melted and the mixture is smooth, then set aside for 5 minutes.

Combine the sugar and water in a medium saucepan and stir over low heat until the sugar has dissolved. Bring to the boil and cook, without stirring, until the mixture is a caramel colour. Pour the caramel into a 20 cm ceramic ovenproof dish and swirl it around to coat the sides.

Whisk the eggs, egg yolks and extra sugar in a medium bowl until well combined. Add the milk mixture and stir until smooth, then pour through a strainer into the baking dish. Place the dish in a baking tray and carefully pour hot water into the tray until it reaches halfway up the sides of the dish. Bake for 1¼ hours or until just set. Remove and allow to cool, then refrigerate for at least 6 hours or overnight.

To serve, run a warm dry knife around the edge of the dish and invert the creme caramel onto a plate.

FEAST FOR MEME

LABNA AND TUNISIAN DUKKAH
WITH PICKLED SPRING VEGETABLES

ZAALOUK (SLOW-COOKED EGGPLANT
AND TOMATO SALAD)

TUNISIAN CARROT AND POTATO SALAD
WITH EGG, GREEN CHILLI AND CAPERS

SPICY LEBANESE-STYLE PEAS
WITH MINCED LAMB

BEEF SHISKABOB

QUINOA, RICE AND TOMATO PILAV

MOROCCAN MESS

4 cups (1.1 kg) thick plain yoghurt

100 ml extra virgin olive oil

warm flatbread and olives, to serve

Pickled spring vegetables

12 dutch (baby) carrots, peeled and trimmed if necessary

1 celery heart, cut into quarters with leaves intact

2 long red chillies, sliced on the diagonal

2 small bulbs fennel, peeled and
    each cut into 8 pieces

10 really small golden shallots

1 tiny savoy cabbage (or ½ small savoy cabbage),
    outer leaves removed and cut into 6–8 wedges

1 spiral green cauliflower, cut into florets

12 mini cucumbers, split down the middle

1 large handful river salt flakes

2 tablespoons mustard seeds

180 g caster sugar

90 g river salt flakes, extra

600 ml white wine vinegar

1 teaspoon black peppercorns

2 fresh bay leaves

4 sprigs thyme

6 cloves garlic, peeled and bruised

1 red chilli, split

Tunisian dukkah

150 g pistachio kernels, chopped

150 g blanched almonds, toasted and crushed

2 tablespoons sesame seeds

2 tablespoons ground coriander

1 tablespoon ground cumin

1 teaspoon coriander seeds, lightly crushed

1 teaspoon cumin seeds

1 teaspoon nigella seeds

1 teaspoon caraway seeds

1 teaspoon ground turmeric

½ teaspoon chilli powder

½ teaspoon freshly ground black pepper

pinch of ground cardamom

pinch of saffron threads

LABNA AND TUNISIAN DUKKAH WITH PICKLED SPRING VEGETABLES

This homemade dukkah is divine – the chilli powder, saffron and turmeric add to its heady fragrance, making it the perfect partner for the creamy labna. Dukkah is great sprinkled on eggs, freshly seared fish or grilled chook. The pickle brine may be used to pickle just about any fresh spring vegetable. You will need to start the labna and pickles a few days before serving.

To prepare the pickled vegetables, place all the vegetables and salt flakes in a large bowl. Using your hands, scrunch everything together really hard to bruise the vegetables and rub the salt through, then weigh down with a plate and set aside for at least 1 hour.

Drain the accumulated water away from the vegetables, then squeeze them to remove any excess liquid. Pack into hot sterilised jars. (I usually wash the jars on the rinse cycle in the dishwasher, then remove while still hot and pack them immediately.)

Combine the remaining ingredients in a medium saucepan and bring to the boil. Reduce the heat and simmer for 4 minutes, then pour the hot liquid over the vegetables in the jars. Gently push the vegetables down so they are completely covered in the liquid and allow to cool. Seal the jars with the lids, then cure in the fridge for at least 2–3 days before eating.

Spoon the yoghurt into a fine sieve lined with a clean Chux or J-cloth. Leave to drain over a bowl for 2 days until the yoghurt is very thick.

To make the dukkah, combine all the ingredients in a dry bowl. Store in an airtight container until needed.

Turn out the labna onto a serving platter and pour the olive oil over the top. Sprinkle generously with dukkah and serve with the pickles, warm flatbread and olives.

Labna and dukkah pictured page 112.

SERVES 6–8

4 large eggplants (aubergines)

12 ripe roma (plum) tomatoes, core removed

200 ml extra virgin olive oil

sea salt and freshly ground black pepper

4 cloves garlic, finely sliced

3 teaspoons cumin seeds

3 teaspoons caraway seeds

2 tablespoons harissa

juice of 1 lemon

½ bunch coriander, leaves picked
   and finely chopped, plus extra leaves to garnish

1 tablespoon nigella seeds

warm flatbread or Turkish bread, to serve

ZAALOUK (SLOW-COOKED EGGPLANT AND TOMATO SALAD)

Half salad, half dip, zaalouk may be enjoyed on its own or as an accompaniment. The slow cooking really intensifies the flavours of the tomato and spices.

Preheat the oven to 200°C (fan-forced). Rest the whole eggplants over a naked gas jet for 3–5 minutes to blacken the skin, then transfer to a baking tray and roast for 15–20 minutes. Remove and leave to cool slightly. Reduce the oven temperature to 130°C (fan-forced).

Cut the eggplants in half lengthways and scoop out the flesh with a spoon. Place the flesh in a baking dish, add the tomatoes and oil and season with lots of salt and pepper. Place the dish in the oven and slow-roast for about an hour.

Remove the baking dish from the oven and set aside for 20 minutes to cool slightly. Pull the skins off the tomatoes with your fingers.

Heat some of the roasting oil from the baking dish in a large frying pan over medium heat and fry the garlic. Grind the spices in a mortar and pestle and add to the pan. Stir in the eggplant flesh and tomatoes and cook for 10 minutes or until thickened. Season to taste with salt and add the harissa, then set aside to cool.

Stir in a little more roasting oil if you think it needs it, then tip into a bowl and drizzle the lemon juice over the top. Stir through the coriander, sprinkle with the nigella seeds and extra coriander and serve with warm bread.

SERVES 6

4 carrots, peeled and sliced on an angle

4 desiree or kipfler potatoes, peeled
   and cut into 2 cm pieces

100 ml extra virgin olive oil

juice of 1 lemon

2 teaspoons ground caraway seeds

1 green chilli, finely chopped

sea salt and freshly ground black pepper

3 large eggs, semi-hard-boiled, peeled
   and cut into quarters

3 tablespoons baby capers

5 radishes, cleaned and cut in half

1 handful salted and dried black olives

sliced green chilli, extra, to serve

80 ml hot chilli sauce, or to taste

lemon wedges, to serve (optional)

TUNISIAN CARROT AND POTATO SALAD WITH EGG, GREEN CHILLI AND CAPERS

When I was a child, my grandmother used to make a salad that combined these unique flavours, and I've loved it ever since. Try it as a light lunch or as part of a selection of salads with a barbecue.

Cook the carrot and potato in lightly salted boiling water for 10–15 minutes or until tender. Drain and cool slightly.

Combine the olive oil, lemon juice, caraway seeds, chilli, salt and pepper in a medium bowl. Add the potato and carrot and toss gently. Spread on a platter and top with the eggs, capers, radishes, olives, extra chilli and hot chilli sauce. Serve with lemon wedges on the side, if desired.

SERVES 6–8

100 ml olive oil

3 onions, finely chopped

5 cloves garlic, finely chopped

450 g lean lamb mince

sea salt and freshly ground black pepper

3 teaspoons mixed spice

2 teaspoons dried chilli flakes

1 tablespoon dried mint

400 g can chopped tomatoes

4 tablespoons tomato paste (puree)

800 ml water

900 g frozen peas

plain yoghurt, to serve (optional)

lemon juice, to serve (optional)

½ bunch mint, leaves picked

SPICY LEBANESE-STYLE PEAS WITH MINCED LAMB

This dish allows the zesty, tomato-flavoured peas to shine. It is just as delicious reheated the next day.

Heat the olive oil in a saucepan over medium heat and cook the onion and garlic for 5 minutes. Add the lamb and cook, stirring frequently, until browned. Stir in the spices, mint, tomato and salt to taste and cook for about 3 minutes. Add the tomato paste, water and peas and cook, partly covered, for 20 minutes.

To serve, dollop the yoghurt over the lamb mixture, add a little lemon juice (if using) and a scattering of mint leaves.

Pictured page 124.

SERVES 6–8

2 brown onions, coarsely grated

2 tablespoons sea salt flakes

1 tablespoon cumin seeds

2 teaspoons caraway seeds

4 cloves garlic

1 teaspoon sea salt flakes, extra

2 teaspoons sweet smoked paprika

2 tablespoons harissa

juice of 2 lemons

½ bunch flat-leaf parsley, leaves picked and chopped

1 bunch coriander, leaves picked and chopped

900 g scotch fillet steak, trimmed and cut into 3 cm cubes

BEEF SHISKABOB

This method of seasoning the onion juice to make a marinade is extraordinarily flavoursome, and the harissa adds a lovely warmth to the dish. Serve with thick plain yoghurt and freshly baked flatbread.

Combine the grated onion and salt flakes in a bowl and leave for 10 minutes. Squeeze out the juice through a clean Chux or J-cloth into a large bowl and discard the solids.

Grind the cumin seeds, caraway seeds, garlic and extra salt flakes in a mortar and pestle, then add the paprika, harissa and lemon juice. Tip the mixture into the onion juice and stir in the chopped herbs. Add the beef and mix really well, then cover and leave to marinate for 4–6 hours.

Thread the beef onto metal skewers and grill for about 3 minutes each side until cooked, but still pink and tender in the middle.

Pictured page 124.

SERVES 6–8

800 g vine-ripened tomatoes,
    peeled and diced
400 ml chicken stock
1 vegetable stock cube
3 tablespoons extra virgin olive oil
80 g butter
4 golden shallots, finely diced
6 cloves garlic, diced
320 g basmati rice, rinsed
200 g quinoa, rinsed
6 sprigs thyme, leaves pulled off
sea salt and freshly ground black pepper

QUINOA, RICE AND TOMATO PILAV

Quinoa is an extremely nutritious, slightly nutty-flavoured grain. This pilav (Turkish for pilau) is a great accompaniment to fish or chicken and can be served hot or cold.

Puree the diced tomato, then place in a small saucepan with the chicken stock and bring to the boil. Add the stock cube and boil for 1 minute, then remove from the heat and set aside.

Heat the olive oil and half the butter in a medium, wide-based saucepan over medium heat and cook the shallot and garlic, stirring, for 2 minutes. Add the rice and quinoa and stir to coat well in the oil and butter. Pour in the tomato stock and bring to a simmer. Stir in the thyme, then reduce the heat to low, cover the pan with a tight-fitting lid and cook for 15 minutes. Remove from the heat. Fork through the remaining butter and season with salt and pepper. Replace the lid and allow to stand for 5 minutes before serving.

Pictured page 124.

Clockwise from top: Beef shiskabob (see page 122), Spicy Lebanese-style peas with minced lamb (see page 122) and Quinoa, rice and tomato pilav (see page 123)

800 ml vanilla ice-cream, softened

4 large meringues (shop bought is fine),
   lightly crushed

2 punnets (500 g) organic strawberries,
   hulled and sliced from tip to top

2 handfuls vanilla Persian fairy floss

Pomegranate jelly

8 leaves gold-strength gelatine

500 ml cranberry juice

100 g glucose syrup

150 ml pomegranate molasses

2 tablespoons cornflour mixed with
   a little cold cranberry juice

MOROCCAN MESS

An exotic take on Eton mess, the well-known dessert of meringue, cream and berries. This version has tangy pomegranate and cranberry jelly stirred through – it tastes so good!

To make the pomegranate jelly, soak the gelatine leaves in cold water until soft, then squeeze to remove any excess water. Combine the cranberry juice, glucose and pomegranate molasses in a super-clean stainless steel saucepan over medium heat. Whisk in the cornflour paste and bring to a simmer, then take the pan off the heat and add the gelatine. Pour into a medium rectangular container and leave to set in the fridge for at least 6 hours or overnight. Loosen the sides with a palette knife, then tip out the jelly onto a clean board and cut into cubes.

Place a few scoops of ice-cream on a platter. Top with a little meringue and stick in some of the strawberry slices. Add another few scoops of ice-cream, a bit more meringue and then the jelly cubes. Add the remaining strawberry slices, ice-cream and meringue, layering the ingredients to form a tower, then swirl around the Persian fairy floss (this can be a bit messy, but the effect is well worth it). Serve immediately.

FEAST OF VEGETABLES AND GRAINS

RICOTTA AND FETA FRITTERS WITH WALNUTS AND YOGHURT SAUCE

SMOKED EGGPLANT SOUP WITH FETA BRUSCHETTA, CUMIN AND CORIANDER OIL

RED KIDNEY BEAN AND CAPSICUM HOTPOT

SWEET QUINOA WITH DRIED APRICOTS, ALMONDS AND ORANGE BLOSSOM WATER

350 g fresh ricotta, well drained

2 small eggs

3 tablespoons plain flour, plus 4 tablespoons extra
    for dusting

freshly ground black pepper

100 g Greek feta, crumbled

extra virgin olive oil, for shallow-frying

½ cup (50 g) walnuts, toasted and coarsely chopped

2 handfuls mint leaves, chopped

Yoghurt sauce

1 cup (280 g) plain yoghurt

¼ clove garlic, chopped

2 tablespoons extra virgin olive oil

juice of ½ lemon

RICOTTA AND FETA FRITTERS WITH WALNUTS AND YOGHURT SAUCE

Ricotta and feta work really well with walnuts. These fritters can be served small, as pictured, or made slightly larger to serve as a meze-style starter.

Combine the ricotta, eggs, flour and pepper in a bowl, then crumble in the feta. Cover and rest in the fridge for 20 minutes.

To make the sauce, combine all the ingredients in a bowl and mix well.

Form 2 tablespoons of the ricotta mixture into each fritter and dust with the extra flour.

Heat a little olive oil in a large non-stick frying pan over medium heat and add a few fritters at a time. Cook for 2 minutes each side or until golden and cooked through. Drain on paper towel.

To serve, spread the sauce over a serving plate, add the fritters and top with the walnuts and mint.

5 eggplants (aubergines)

100 ml extra virgin olive oil

5 golden shallots, finely sliced

4 cloves garlic, finely chopped

1 litre chicken or vegetable stock

200 ml pouring cream

sea salt and freshly ground black pepper

100 g feta, sliced

4 slices sourdough bread, toasted and roughly torn

Coriander oil

1 bunch coriander, leaves picked

1 teaspoon ground cumin

4 tablespoons extra virgin olive oil

½ clove garlic

freshly ground black pepper

SMOKED EGGPLANT SOUP WITH FETA BRUSCHETTA, CUMIN AND CORIANDER OIL

The rich smoked flavour in this comforting soup is unexpected yet utterly delicious.

Preheat the oven to 200°C (fan-forced).

Place the eggplants on a barbecue or open flame and cook, turning frequently, until the skin is black. Transfer to the oven and roast for 15 minutes or until soft. Cool, then cut them in half, scoop out the flesh and coarsely chop.

Heat the olive oil in a wide saucepan over medium heat and cook the shallot and garlic for 2–3 minutes. Add the chopped eggplant and cook, stirring, for 2 minutes. Pour in the chicken or vegetable stock and bring to a simmer. Cook for 2–3 minutes, then add the cream. Season with salt and pepper and bring back to a simmer. Allow to cool slightly, then process in a blender or food processor until smooth.

To make the coriander oil, combine all the ingredients in a blender and process until smooth (or you can do this in a mortar and pestle).

To serve, ladle the hot soup into bowls and drizzle with coriander oil. Spread the feta over the toasted sourdough and place on top of the soup or serve on the side.

Pictured page 128.

100 ml extra virgin olive oil

2 red capsicums (peppers), seeds removed,
  cut into 2 cm pieces

2 large chillies, sliced diagonally

1 carrot, peeled and finely diced

3 sticks celery, finely diced

2 leeks, cut into 1 cm slices

4 cloves garlic, sliced

2 brown onions, finely diced

sea salt and freshly ground black pepper

1 teaspoon sweet smoked paprika

1 tablespoon fenugreek seeds

1 tablespoon fennel seeds

5 sprigs thyme

1 bay leaf

2 × 400 g cans red kidney beans, drained and rinsed

400 g can chickpeas, drained and rinsed

400 g can crushed tomatoes

3 tablespoons tomato paste (puree)

1 avocado

juice of 1 lime

3 tablespoons coriander leaves

steamed brown rice, to serve

sheep's milk yoghurt, to serve

RED KIDNEY BEAN AND CAPSICUM HOTPOT

This hearty and filling hotpot makes you feel healthy and well-nourished. It gets better over time, so make it a few days in advance to let the flavours develop.

Heat the olive oil in a large saucepan over medium heat and cook the capsicum and chilli for 10 minutes. Add the carrot, celery, leek, garlic, onion, salt, spices and herbs and cook for about 25 minutes or until the mixture is caramelised. Add the kidney beans and chickpeas and season with salt and pepper, then stir in the tomatoes and tomato paste. Add enough water to just cover and simmer over low heat for 30 minutes.

Dice the avocado and toss with the lime juice and coriander. Season with salt.

To serve, spoon the hotpot over steamed brown rice and dollop with yoghurt. Top with the avocado and coriander mixture.

Pictured pages 134–135.

Red kidney bean and capsicum hotpot
(see page 133)

SERVES 8

140 g dried apricots

140 g prunes

3 tablespoons sultanas

100 g caster sugar

1 tablespoon orange blossom water

1 tablespoon lemon juice

3 tablespoons unsalted pistachio kernels

3 tablespoons blanched almonds, toasted and chopped

100 g fresh pomegranate seeds

300 g quinoa

1 tablespoon vegetable oil

300 ml milk

2 tablespoons caster sugar, extra

100 g unsalted butter, softened

3 unsprayed pink roses, to garnish (optional)

300 g plain yoghurt

1½ teaspoons rosewater

SWEET QUINOA WITH DRIED APRICOTS, ALMONDS AND ORANGE BLOSSOM WATER

Sweet quinoa should be made with the finest grain you can find. Serve this rich dessert warm and in small portions. Orange blossom water and rosewater are available at selected supermarkets, health-food stores and delicatessens.

Soak the dried apricots and prunes in hot water for 20 minutes, and the sultanas for 5 minutes. Drain.

Combine the sugar with 250 ml water in a saucepan and bring to the boil over high heat. Add the apricots, prunes and sultanas, then reduce the heat and simmer for 5 minutes. Remove the pan from the heat and stir in the orange blossom water and lemon juice. Add the nuts and pomegranate seeds, stir well and set aside.

Combine the quinoa and oil in a bowl. Place the milk, extra sugar and 350 ml water in a medium saucepan over medium heat and bring to the boil. Pour in the quinoa and simmer, stirring, for 10–15 minutes or until tender (you may need to add a little more milk). Cover and set aside for 5 minutes. Add the butter and stir well with a fork.

Press the quinoa into a bowl, then turn out onto a platter. Spoon the fruit mixture around and over the quinoa. Garnish with rose petals if you like.

Mix together the yoghurt and rosewater and serve with the quinoa.

MIDDLE EASTERN LUNCH

PRAWN AND WATERMELON SALAD
WITH FETA, MINT AND POMEGRANATE

CRISPY FRIED LAMB WITH CHICKPEA PUREE
AND CARROT AND BEETROOT SALAD

TURKISH CHICKEN WITH APRICOTS,
SAFFRON AND PISTACHIOS

TOFFEE-DIPPED DATES STUFFED
WITH ALMONDS AND CHOCOLATE

24 cooked tiger prawns, peeled and deveined

½ red onion, sliced

2 tablespoons ground sumac

sea salt and freshly ground black pepper

2 tablespoons olive oil

¼ watermelon (about 2 kg), skin removed

3 tablespoons fresh pomegranate seeds

5 sprigs mint, leaves picked and torn

5 sprigs coriander, leaves picked and torn

2 pinches of chilli powder

80 g feta, crumbled

3 tablespoons extra virgin olive oil

1½ tablespoons sherry vinegar

1 tablespoon pomegranate molasses

PRAWN AND WATERMELON SALAD WITH FETA, MINT AND POMEGRANATE

The fresh, sweet flavour of melon, the saltiness of feta and the sharpness of pomegranate wake up the palate, making a great start to this Middle Eastern feast.

Toss the prawns and red onion in the sumac, salt and 1 tablespoon olive oil until well coated.

Slice half the watermelon into 1.5 cm pieces, then into triangles and arrange on a platter. Sprinkle the onion and prawns over the top, then scatter over the pomegranate seeds, herbs and chilli powder. Season with salt and pepper and dot with feta.

Combine the olive oil, vinegar and pomegranate molasses and spoon over the salad.

Pictured page 142.

300 g lamb mince

1 teaspoon ground cumin

1 teaspoon ground coriander

½ teaspoon chilli flakes

1 teaspoon sea salt

1 teaspoon ground ginger

warm Turkish bread, to serve

Chickpea puree

2 × 400 g cans chickpeas

1 bay leaf

2 cloves garlic, halved

100 ml extra virgin olive oil

2 teaspoons tahini paste

juice of 2 lemons

1–2 tablespoons hot water (optional)

Carrot and beetroot salad

2 carrots, peeled and sliced lengthways
    really thinly with a peeler or mandolin

2 beetroot, peeled and cut into matchsticks

5 sprigs coriander, leaves picked

4 sprigs mint, leaves picked

1 small red chilli, finely sliced

juice of 1 lemon

1 teaspoon sugar

2½ tablespoons extra virgin olive oil

sea salt and freshly ground black pepper

CRISPY FRIED LAMB WITH CHICKPEA PUREE AND CARROT AND BEETROOT SALAD

Step aside plain old hummus – this is the fanciest, tastiest dip you'll ever come across.

For the puree, place the chickpeas and bay leaf in a saucepan of water over medium heat and bring to the boil. Drain. Puree the hot chickpeas and garlic in a food processor. Add the remaining ingredients and process until smooth, adding a little hot water, if necessary.

To make the carrot and beetroot salad, place all the ingredients in a bowl and toss gently to combine.

Place the lamb mince in a non-stick frying pan over high heat and cook for 8–10 minutes until brown, then add the spices and cook for 1 minute.

To serve, spoon the chickpea puree onto a platter. Pile the salad on the side with the lamb and serve with warm Turkish bread.

Pictured page 143.

Prawn and watermelon salad with feta, mint and
pomegranate (see page 140)

Crispy fried lamb with chickpea puree and carrot and beetroot salad (see page 141)

2 teaspoons sea salt

2 teaspoons ground cumin

2 teaspoons ground coriander

2 teaspoons ground cinnamon

1 teaspoon freshly ground black pepper

2 teaspoons ground turmeric

2 teaspoons dried chilli flakes

1.8 kg free-range chicken, cut into 8 pieces

100 ml olive oil

1 brown onion, chopped

100 g fresh ginger, cut into matchsticks

6 cloves garlic, crushed

2 green chillies, split

3 tablespoons tomato paste (puree)

2 pinches of saffron threads

5 sprigs thyme, leaves picked

200 ml white wine

200 g dried apricots

finely grated zest and juice of 1 lemon

2 tablespoons honey

2 tablespoons vegetable stock powder

1 handful pistachio kernels, plus extra
   to garnish (optional)

mint leaves, to garnish (optional)

steamed couscous, to serve

plain yoghurt, to serve

TURKISH CHICKEN WITH APRICOTS, SAFFRON AND PISTACHIOS

This recipe is a world away from the apricot chicken my mum made in the 1970s. This version has great depth of flavour with a delicate blend of Turkish spices and fresh apricots.

Combine the salt, cumin, coriander, cinnamon, pepper, turmeric and chilli flakes in a large plastic bag. Add the chicken pieces and shake to coat.

Heat the olive oil in a large heavy-based wide saucepan over high heat. Brown the chicken on all sides, then remove from the pan and set aside. Add the onion, ginger, garlic and green chillies and cook for about 3 minutes, adding a little more oil, if necessary. Stir in the tomato paste, saffron and thyme and cook for 1 minute.

Add the wine and dried apricots and bring to a simmer. Stir in the lemon zest, lemon juice, honey and stock powder and return the chicken to the pan. Pour in enough water to just cover the chicken and simmer, covered, over medium heat for 10 minutes. Uncover and simmer for a further 10–15 minutes or until the chicken is tender and cooked through. Stir in the pistachios.

Garnish with mint leaves and extra pistachios if liked and serve with steamed couscous and plain yoghurt.

MAKES 10

150 g dark chocolate
50 g butter, chopped
120 ml pouring cream
4 pinches of sea salt flakes
10 large fresh dates
10 toasted almonds
350 g caster sugar
125 ml water

TOFFEE-DIPPED DATES STUFFED WITH ALMONDS AND CHOCOLATE

Enough with all that healthy food! You must try these tiny but naughty treats. The salty chocolate is an unexpected but perfect partner for the sweet toffee. The dates look very pretty served in foil cases but of course these are optional.

Melt the chocolate in a large heatproof bowl over a saucepan of barely simmering water (don't let the bowl touch the water). Combine the warm chocolate with the butter, cream and salt and stir until smooth. Cool to room temperature.

Run a knife along the length of each date and slip the pit out, taking care not to squash the dates. Use a teaspoon to fill the dates with the chocolate mixture. Place an almond in each, then press gently to close. Transfer to a plate and refrigerate for 1 hour.

Combine the sugar and water in a small saucepan and stir over low heat until the sugar has dissolved. Increase the heat and boil, without stirring, until the mixture turns a caramel colour. Remove from the heat and cool for 1 minute. Tilt the saucepan slightly and carefully dip the dates in the toffee, turning to coat, then place on baking paper to cool and set. Serve in foil cases if liked.

MIDDLE EASTERN DINNER

ZA'ATAR-DUSTED RICOTTA AND HALOUMI
PASTRIES WITH POMEGRANATE MOLASSES

ROAST CHICKEN WITH CORIANDER SEEDS,
THYME AND CHERRY TOMATOES

BROAD BEANS WITH GARLIC AND HARISSA

BABY POTATOES WITH SOUR CREAM,
PISTACHIOS AND DILL

POACHED APRICOTS WITH ORANGE BLOSSOM
CREAM AND APPLE VERBENA JELLY

2 eggs

275 g ricotta, well drained

150 g haloumi, grated

3 tablespoons frozen peas, rinsed in hot water, drained

20 mint leaves, chopped

1½ tablespoons dried mint

1 handful dried breadcrumbs

sea salt and freshly ground black pepper

375 g filo pastry

150 g unsalted butter, melted

3 tablespoons za'atar

3 tablespoons pomegranate molasses

ZA'ATAR-DUSTED RICOTTA AND HALOUMI PASTRIES WITH POMEGRANATE MOLASSES

These are quite fiddly but well worth the effort. The pomegranate molasses drizzles to the bottom of the pastries, creating little parcels of yumminess.

Preheat the oven to 180°C (fan-forced).

Place one egg and one egg yolk in a bowl (reserve the white for later). Add the ricotta, haloumi, peas, fresh and dried mint, breadcrumbs, salt and pepper and stir to combine.

Spread out one pastry sheet on a large cutting board and brush with melted butter. Place another sheet on top, then cut horizontally into four strips. Sit two strips on top of the other two strips to form two lengths. Place 1 tablespoon of the filling on the end of each strip and fold the pastry over to form a triangle. Keep folding all the way up each strip to form two sealed triangles. Brush a little egg white on the ends of the pastry to seal. Repeat with the remaining pastry sheets and filling to make about 20 triangles.

Place the triangles on a non-stick baking tray, brushing with the remaining butter and sprinkling with za'atar as you go. Bake for 15 minutes or until golden.

Arrange the pastries on a platter, drizzle over the pomegranate molasses and serve.

Pictured page 148.

SERVES 4

3 tablespoons coriander seeds

1 tablespoon black peppercorns

8 cloves garlic, unpeeled

1½ teaspoons dried chilli flakes

2 tablespoons flaked river salt

1.8 kg free-range organic chicken,
   cut into 8 pieces

1½ tablespoons extra virgin olive oil

8 sprigs thyme

12 cherry tomatoes

2 tablespoons sherry vinegar

ROAST CHICKEN WITH CORIANDER SEEDS, THYME AND CHERRY TOMATOES

The chilli and herb marinade gives the chicken
a fragrant kick. Because of the way the chicken is
chopped, it caramelises beautifully. It's important to
have a big enough pan to allow this process to happen.
The tomatoes give this dish a great burst of flavour.

Roughly crush the coriander seeds and peppercorns
in a mortar and pestle, then add the garlic and roughly
crush. Add the chilli flakes and salt and pound to a
rough paste. Place the chicken pieces in a large plastic
bag, add the spice mix and olive oil and massage
into the chicken. Refrigerate for at least 15 minutes
(overnight if possible) to allow the flavours to infuse.

Preheat the oven to 220°C (fan-forced).

Remove the chicken from the bag and place in a
medium heavy baking dish. Scatter over the thyme
sprigs and tomatoes and roast for 55 minutes or until
the chicken is golden and cooked.

Remove the dish from the oven, drizzle over the vinegar
and allow to rest for 5 minutes. Serve the chicken with
the pan juices spooned over.

Pictured page 152.

3 cloves garlic, unpeeled

2 kg broad beans, shelled to make 3 cups

1 cup (120 g) frozen baby peas

2 teaspoons cumin seeds

100 ml extra virgin olive oil, plus extra to serve

1 teaspoon black peppercorns, coarsely ground

2 tablespoons harissa

½ lemon

sea salt

1 kg small chat (baby) potatoes,
    such as kipfler or pink-eye

3 tablespoons sour cream

1 tablespoon extra virgin olive oil

4 tablespoons pistachio kernels

2 tablespoons chopped dill

2 spring onions, finely sliced

BROAD BEANS WITH GARLIC AND HARISSA

This recipe is inspired by a dish made by my Tunisian grandmother.

Bring 1.25 litres lightly salted water to the boil, add the garlic cloves and boil for 10 minutes over high heat. Add the broad beans and cook for 2 minutes. Drain and cool slightly, reserving the garlic. Peel the large broad beans and leave the small beans unpeeled.

Blanch the peas for 1 minute, then drain and add to the broad beans. Squeeze the garlic from the skins, then mash and add to the broad bean mixture.

Combine the cumin seeds, olive oil and peppercorns in a mortar and pestle and pound until smooth. Add the cumin mixture, harissa and a squeeze of lemon juice to the broad beans and peas and stir to combine. Drizzle with a little extra olive oil and sprinkle with sea salt before serving.

BABY POTATOES WITH SOUR CREAM, PISTACHIOS AND DILL

This nutty potato salad is great with the roast chicken.

Cook the potatoes in lightly salted boiling water until tender and the skins start to split. Drain and allow to cool slightly, then slip off the skins. Cool to room temperature, then stir through the sour cream and olive oil.

Finely chop the pistachio kernels to resemble fresh breadcrumbs. Place in a bowl with the dill and spring onion and mix together well. Sprinkle over the baby potatoes and serve.

SERVES 8

180 ml white wine

⅔ cup (150 g) caster sugar

½ vanilla bean, split, seeds scraped
   and cut into fine splinters

8 small ripe apricots, stone removed
   and halved

juice of ½ lemon

½ sponge cake (bought is fine)

2 tablespoons icing sugar

Apple verbena jelly

500 ml clear apple juice

2 sprigs lemon verbena, leaves picked

5 leaves gold-strength gelatine

Orange blossom cream

150 ml thickened cream

2 teaspoons orange blossom water

POACHED APRICOTS WITH ORANGE BLOSSOM CREAM AND APPLE VERBENA JELLY

You could set this jelly with blueberries or lychees if apricots are out of season – just cook the wine and sugar mixture for half the time. If you can't find lemon verbena at your greengrocer, a seedling from a nursery is a good option. Otherwise, it's fine to leave it out.

Place the wine and sugar in a small saucepan over medium heat and bring to a simmer. Add the vanilla bean splinters, apricots and lemon juice and simmer for 5 minutes, then turn off the heat and allow the apricots to cool in the juice.

To make the apple verbena jelly, heat the apple juice over medium heat in a small saucepan until warm. Remove from the heat, add the lemon verbena and set aside to infuse for about 15 minutes. Meanwhile, soak the gelatine leaves in cold water until soft, then squeeze to remove any excess water.

Strain the apple juice through a sieve into a jug, discarding the leaves. Return 2½ tablespoons of the juice to the saucepan and warm over medium heat. Add the gelatine and remove from the heat. Stir to dissolve, then add the remaining apple juice. Pour the liquid evenly into eight glasses and drop two apricot halves into each. Refrigerate for 2–3 hours or until set.

To make the orange blossom cream, whip the cream to stiff peaks, then fold in the orange blossom water. Cover and place in the fridge.

Cut the sponge cake into 1.5 cm thick slices, then cut out eight tiny rounds. Dust each round with icing sugar.

Remove the glasses from the fridge and top with a dollop of orange blossom cream. Finish with a sponge round and serve.

SPECIAL OCCASION DINNER

WATERCRESS, PEA AND POTATO
SOUP WITH CRUMBED OYSTERS

ORANGE, TOMATO AND PARSLEY SALAD
WITH CELERY SEEDS AND GREEN CHILLI

ROAST SPATCHCOCK WITH CHORIZO,
TOMATO AND YELLOW PEA PASTE

HONEYCOMB

CRUSHED HONEYCOMB AND
FROMAGE FRAIS PANNA COTTA

SERVES 4–6

2½ tablespoons extra virgin olive oil

50 g butter

5 cloves garlic, sliced

6 golden shallots, sliced

1 leek, finely sliced

300 g desiree potatoes, peeled and finely sliced

750 ml fish stock

250 ml water

1½ cups (180 g) frozen peas

1 bunch watercress, leaves picked and chopped,
    plus extra sprigs to garnish

150 g baby spinach leaves

200 ml pouring cream

sea salt and freshly ground black pepper

1 tablespoon vermouth

juice of ½ lemon

Crumbed oysters

¾ cup (110 g) plain flour

1 egg, lightly beaten

1 cup (70 g) fresh or Japanese panko breadcrumbs

12 Pacific oysters, freshly shucked, drained
    on paper towel

50 g unsalted butter

2½ tablespoons extra virgin olive oil

sea salt and freshly ground black pepper

juice of ½ lemon

WATERCRESS, PEA AND POTATO SOUP WITH CRUMBED OYSTERS

This soup is silky smooth and the crumbed oysters are crispy, briny and delightful.

Heat the olive oil and butter in a large heavy-based saucepan over medium heat and cook the garlic, shallot and leek, stirring frequently, for 5–8 minutes without colouring.

Add the potato and cook for 6 minutes. Pour in the fish stock and water and simmer for 12–15 minutes or until the vegetables are tender. Add the peas, watercress and spinach and cook for 4 minutes, then stir in the cream and cook for 2 minutes. Place the soup in a food processor or blender and process until smooth (or use a stick blender). Taste and adjust the seasoning if necessary, then stir in the vermouth.

For the crumbed oysters, place the flour, egg and breadcrumbs in three small bowls. Dip the oysters into the flour, then the egg, and then the breadcrumbs, shaking off any excess. Heat the butter and olive oil in a small frying pan. Add the oysters (in batches if necessary) and cook for 30 seconds each side or until golden. Season with salt and pepper and squeeze over the lemon juice.

To serve, spoon the soup into bowls, add the oysters and a squeeze of lemon juice and garnish with the extra watercress sprigs (or fennel fronds, if you have some to hand).

Pictured page 156.

SERVES 6–8

4 oranges

2 ripe tomatoes, finely chopped

½ bunch flat-leaf parsley, leaves picked
   and chopped

2 green chillies, finely chopped

2 teaspoons celery seeds

1 clove garlic, finely chopped

100 ml extra virgin olive oil

juice of ½ lemon

1¼ tablespoons sherry vinegar

½ red onion, finely chopped

sea salt and freshly ground black pepper

ORANGE, TOMATO AND PARSLEY SALAD WITH CELERY SEEDS AND GREEN CHILLI

This salad is perfect with the roast spatchcock – the orange zest gives it a lovely depth and bitterness. Be sure to use full-flavoured tomatoes.

Finely grate the zest from one orange, then remove the pith and cut into segments. Segment two other oranges. Cut the remaining orange into rounds, (pith on) and then into small triangles.

Place the orange zest, segments and triangles in a bowl with the remaining ingredients, season to taste and toss gently. Allow to rest for about 15 minutes before serving.

Pictured page 160.

Orange, tomato and parsley salad with celery seeds and green chilli (see page 159)

Roast spatchcock with chorizo, tomato and yellow pea paste (see page 163)

SERVES 8

1 cup (200 g) yellow split peas

2 cloves garlic

1 bay leaf

1 small potato, peeled and sliced

180 ml extra virgin olive oil

sea salt and freshly ground black pepper

4 spatchcocks, back bone removed and flattened

1 chorizo sausage, thinly sliced

4 sprigs oregano

butter, for pan-frying

6 golden shallots, peeled and thickly sliced

1 bulb garlic, cloves separated and lightly crushed

2 red chillies, split

1½ tablespoons sherry vinegar

250 ml chicken stock

flat-leaf parsley sprigs, to garnish (optional)

ROAST SPATCHCOCK WITH CHORIZO, TOMATO AND YELLOW PEA PASTE

Stuffing chorizo under the skin will season the spatchcocks beautifully as they cook.

Combine the split peas, garlic, bay leaf and potato in a saucepan and cover with water. Bring to the boil over medium heat and cook for 25–35 minutes or until the peas are tender. Drain, reserving some of the cooking liquid. Place the peas and 100 ml of the olive oil in a food processor, season to taste and process until smooth, adding a little cooking liquid if necessary to make a semi-smooth paste.

Preheat the oven to 220°C (fan-forced).

Carefully loosen the skin of the spatchcocks to make pockets and insert four to six slices of chorizo and a sprig of oregano in each. Season with salt and pepper.

Heat the remaining olive oil in a large ovenproof frying pan or flameproof baking dish over high heat. Add the spatchcocks and brown on both sides. Add a knob of butter, the shallots, garlic cloves and chilli and cook for 3 minutes. Stir in the vinegar, bring to the boil and simmer for 10 seconds. Pour in the chicken stock and boil for 2 minutes, then transfer the pan or dish to the oven and roast the spatchcocks for 8–10 minutes or until cooked and golden.

To serve, spoon the split pea paste onto plates and top with the spatchcocks. Bring the pan juices to the boil over medium heat. Cook, stirring, until the mixture has reduced to a sauce consistency, then pour over the spatchcocks. Garnish with the parsley sprigs, if using, and serve with the yellow pea paste.

MAKES ABOUT 400 G

3 tablespoons water

50 g raw sugar

250 g caster sugar

100 g liquid glucose

4 tablespoons honey

15 g bicarbonate of soda, sifted
    (to prevent lumps through the honeycomb)

SERVES 6–8

4 leaves gold-strength gelatine

250 ml milk

400 ml pouring cream

130 g caster sugar

½ teaspoon vanilla extract

280 g fromage frais

1 large punnet (200 g) ripe raspberries

100 g honeycomb (see recipe, left),
    roughly crushed

HONEYCOMB

To keep it from going sticky and soft, store honeycomb in an airtight container – it will keep in the freezer for up to two weeks. Liquid glucose is available from most supermarkets. You will need a sugar thermometer for this recipe.

Line a tray at least 40 cm wide × 60 cm long × 4 cm deep with baking paper.

Place the water, sugars, glucose and honey in a large, clean stainless-steel saucepan (about 30 cm diameter) over low heat and cook, stirring, until the sugars have dissolved. Increase the heat to medium and cook for about 8 minutes until the mixture reaches 120°C on a sugar thermometer, is a medium-caramel colour and the large bubbles have subsided.

Remove the pan from the heat and quickly whisk in the bicarbonate of soda. The toffee will swell like molten lava, so pour it into the tray very quickly and allow to set for 15–30 minutes. (If the honeycomb has not begun to harden at this stage, the sugar mixture did not cook for long enough and will not set.)

Crack the honeycomb into large shards and serve.

CRUSHED HONEYCOMB AND FROMAGE FRAIS PANNA COTTA >

The fromage frais and raspberries bring a slightly tart note to this dessert, which works beautifully with the sweetness of the panna cotta and honeycomb. This dish is a real knockout.

Soak the gelatine leaves in cold water until soft, then squeeze to remove any excess water.

Place the milk, cream and sugar in a medium saucepan and gently warm over medium heat, but do not allow to boil. Remove the pan from the heat. Add the vanilla and gelatine and stir until the gelatine has dissolved, then strain into a clean bowl. Set aside to cool.

Stir in the fromage frais and pour into six or eight 150 ml dariole moulds. Refrigerate for about 4 hours or until set.

To serve, quickly dip the moulds in hot water and turn out the panna cotta onto plates. Place the raspberries in a bowl and bruise slightly with the back of a spoon. Scatter the raspberries over the panna cotta and sprinkle with the crushed honeycomb.

ASIAN BANQUET

PORK DUMPLINGS WITH SHIITAKE AND GINGER

SALT AND PEPPER SQUID

NOODLES WITH ROAST DUCK AND HOISIN SAUCE

CORIANDER AND OYSTER OMELETTE

STIR-FRIED ASPARAGUS WITH TOFU,
WOMBOK AND ALMONDS

STEAMED EGGPLANT

LIME AND CHICKEN BEAN THREAD NOODLES

SLOW-ROASTED PORK BELLY WITH CUCUMBER,
CORIANDER AND SESAME SPICED DRESSING

40 round wonton wrappers

3 tablespoons vegetable oil

300 ml hot water

Pork and prawn filling

200 g raw prawn meat, chopped

200 g fatty pork belly, finely minced

1 × 227 g can water chestnuts, chopped

1 tablespoon grated ginger

3 spring onions, finely sliced

2 tablespoons oyster sauce

½ teaspoon sesame oil

1 tablespoon light soy sauce

12 shiitake mushrooms, stems removed,
   finely sliced

Dipping sauce

120 ml light soy sauce

2 small red chillies, finely chopped

4 cm piece ginger, cut into superfine matchsticks

1 teaspoon sugar

½ teaspoon sesame oil

PORK AND PRAWN DUMPLINGS WITH SHIITAKE AND GINGER

These tasty morsels can be made ahead of time and frozen.

To make the filling, blend the prawn meat and pork mince in a food processor, then stir through the remaining ingredients.

Spread four wonton wrappers on a clean work surface and moisten the top side with a little water. Place 2–3 teaspoons of the filling in the centre and fold to seal, forming small pleats. Repeat with the remaining wrappers and filling, place on a tray and chill until needed. (The dumplings can be frozen at this stage.)

Heat half the vegetable oil in a large wok over medium heat. Add half the dumplings and cook for 2 minutes each side or until golden. Add half the hot water (take care as the mixture will spit) and cook, covered, for about 5–6 minutes or until the dumplings are ready. Repeat with the remaining oil, dumplings and water.

To make the dipping sauce, combine all the ingredients in a small bowl.

Serve the dumplings with the dipping sauce.

Pictured page 166.

4½ tablespoons cornflour

4 tablespoons plain flour

2 tablespoons crushed Sichuan peppercorns

1 tablespoon sea salt

2 teaspoons Chinese five-spice powder

750 g squid, cleaned, legs and wings retained,
   cut into rings

vegetable oil, for deep-frying

3 handfuls basil leaves

2 large red chillies, sliced on the diagonal

½ iceberg lettuce, shredded

1 lemon, cut into wedges (optional)

SALT AND PEPPER SQUID

For best results, use fresh squid and make sure it is
completely free from water before you dust it for frying.

Combine the flours, peppercorns, salt and five-spice
powder in a large plastic bag. Add the squid and toss
to coat, then remove and shake off any excess.

Pour the vegetable oil in a large wok to a depth of
5–8 cm and heat over high heat until hot. Add the
basil leaves and chilli and cook for about 30 seconds
or until crisp. Remove with a slotted spoon and drain.
Reserve for later.

Add the squid to the wok in batches and cook for
2 minutes or until lightly golden. Drain on paper towel.

To serve, spread the lettuce on a platter, top with
the squid and scatter with the chilli and basil leaves.
Serve with lemon wedges (if using).

Pictured page 171.

Salt and pepper squid (see page 169)

SERVES 2–4

6 large eggs

¼ bunch coriander, leaves picked

1½ tablespoons light soy sauce

2 teaspoons fish sauce

¼ teaspoon sesame oil

2 tablespoons water

2 tablespoons extra virgin olive oil

12 Pacific oysters, shucked and detached
   from the shell

2 spring onions, finely sliced

1 large red chilli, sliced

1 handful bean sprouts

1 tablespoon fried shallots

2 tablespoons hoisin sauce

lime cheeks, to serve

CORIANDER AND OYSTER OMELETTE

This spankingly bright Asian-style omelette is also great for a quick lunch, brunch or starter.

Combine the eggs, coriander, soy sauce, fish sauce, sesame oil and water in a bowl and whisk lightly with a fork.

Heat the olive oil in a large frying pan over high heat for 1 minute. Stir-fry the oysters for 1 minute, then remove from the pan. Add the egg mixture and cook for 30 seconds, scraping the edges to the middle of the pan. Reduce the heat and add the spring onion and push into the egg mixture with a spatula. Scatter the chilli over the top and cook for 1–2 minutes until the omelette is almost firm, then slide onto a plate.

Top with the oysters, bean sprouts and fried shallots, drizzle with hoisin sauce and finish with a squeeze of lime juice. Serve immediately.

2 tablespoons soy sauce

1 teaspoon sesame oil

2 teaspoons sugar

2 tablespoons oyster sauce

4 tablespoons Shaoxing rice wine

4 tablespoons peanut or vegetable oil

3 bunches asparagus, trimmed and sliced diagonally

6 cloves garlic, sliced

3 cm piece ginger, cut into matchsticks

2 large red chillies, sliced diagonally

½ cup (80 g) almonds, toasted and coarsely chopped

4–5 spring onions, cut into 3 cm batons

10 large oyster mushrooms, cut in half

200 g firm tofu, diced

½ small wombok (Chinese cabbage), sliced

½ bunch coriander, leaves picked

STIR-FRIED ASPARAGUS WITH TOFU, WOMBOK AND ALMONDS

I often cook this when I'm in need of a vegetable hit (no rice required). The crunch of the toasted almonds makes it very moreish.

Combine the soy sauce, sesame oil, sugar, oyster sauce and rice wine in a small bowl and set aside.

Heat the oil in a large wok over high heat. When the oil is hot and shimmering, add the asparagus and stir-fry for 2 minutes. Add the garlic, ginger, chilli and almonds and cook for 1 minute, then toss in the spring onion and mushrooms and cook for 30 seconds.

Add the soy sauce mixture, tofu and wombok and stir-fry for 1 minute. Garnish with the coriander and serve immediately.

SERVES 4

½ Chinese roast duck

250 g fresh hokkien noodles

250 g fresh thin egg noodles

3 tablespoons light soy sauce

3 teaspoons sesame oil

120 ml oyster sauce

100 ml hoisin sauce

2 pinches of Chinese five-spice powder

4 tablespoons peanut or vegetable oil

5 cm piece ginger, thinly sliced

6 cloves garlic, sliced

2 long red chillies, sliced diagonally

½ small wombok (Chinese cabbage),
   cut across in 3 cm slices

5 spring onions, cut into 3 cm batons

250 g bean sprouts

½ cup coriander leaves

NOODLES WITH ROAST DUCK AND HOISIN SAUCE

Chinese roast duck is available from specialist Asian shops and some restaurants, or try the Luv-a-Duck range, which you'll find at selected supermarkets and poultry suppliers.

Preheat the oven to 200°C (fan-forced).

Reheat the duck in the oven for 15 minutes, then remove and pull the meat from the bones. Slice and set aside.

Gently loosen the noodles and place in a large heatproof bowl. Cover with boiling water and stand for 1 minute, then drain and refresh under cold water. Drain again and then set aside.

Combine the soy sauce, sesame oil, oyster sauce, hoisin sauce and five-spice powder in a bowl and set aside.

Heat the oil in a large wok over high heat. When the oil is hot and shimmering, add the ginger and garlic and stir-fry for 30 seconds. Add the duck meat and stir-fry for 1–2 minutes. Add the chilli, wombok and spring onion and cook for 30 seconds. Stir in the soy sauce mixture, noodles and bean sprouts, scatter over the coriander and serve immediately.

SERVES 4 AS A SIDE DISH

3 eggplants (aubergines)

sea salt

6 shiitake mushrooms, stems removed

4 spring onions, sliced

2 tablespoons fried shallots

1 large red chilli, finely sliced

Sauce

125 ml Chinese black vinegar

4 tablespoons brown sugar

4 tablespoons light soy sauce

1 teaspoon sesame oil

2 tablespoons Shaoxing rice wine (or sherry)

1 red chilli, split down the middle

STEAMED EGGPLANT WITH BLACK VINEGAR AND SHIITAKE

Kylie Kwong's delicious version of steamed eggplant inspired me to give it a try – cooked this way, the eggplant is wonderfully slippery and silky. Fried shallots and Shaoxing rice wine can be found at Asian food stores.

Cut the eggplants into 1.5 cm slices, then into sticks about 1.5 cm thick. Sprinkle the eggplant with salt and set aside for 10 minutes. Rinse and pat dry.

Place the eggplant and mushrooms in a large steamer and steam for 6–9 minutes or until the vegetables are tender (you may need to do this in batches). Remove and rest for 2–3 minutes. Transfer to a platter and scatter with the spring onion, fried shallots and chilli.

To make the sauce, combine all the ingredients in a small saucepan. Stir over low heat until the sugar has dissolved, then simmer for about 3 minutes or until syrupy.

Pour the sauce over the vegetables and serve.

SERVES 4

140 g bean thread vermicelli

2½ tablespoons vegetable oil

2 cloves garlic, finely sliced

2 large red chillies, finely sliced

350 g minced chicken

1 tablespoon tom yum paste

4 kaffir lime leaves, very finely shredded

4 tablespoons grated palm sugar

2 tablespoons fish sauce, or to taste

150 ml coconut cream

juice of 2 small limes

180 g bean sprouts

½ bunch coriander, leaves picked

15 Thai basil leaves

4 tablespoons peanuts, toasted and chopped

2–3 tablespoons fried shallots

THAI-INSPIRED LIME AND CHICKEN BEAN THREAD NOODLES

This traditional Thai-style noodle salad has a great lime zing with just the right amount of chilli. It makes an ideal side or starter.

Boil the vermicelli in water for 1–2 minutes, then drain and rinse.

Heat the oil in a large frying pan or wok over medium heat and stir-fry the garlic and chilli until aromatic. Add the chicken and cook for about 4 minutes or until the chicken is almost cooked through, breaking up any lumps as you go. Add the tom yum paste, kaffir lime leaves and palm sugar and season with fish sauce. Stir in the coconut cream.

Remove the pan from the heat and add the vermicelli, lime juice, bean sprouts, coriander and basil. Toss to combine, then serve topped with the peanuts and fried shallots.

SERVES 6

1.5 kg piece organic pork belly, thick end
    and bones removed

2 tablespoons vegetable oil

3 tablespoons salt flakes, plus extra to serve

750 ml water

2 large cucumbers, peeled, seeded and sliced into
    5 mm thick rounds (run a fork down the side
    to make grooves if you like)

½ bunch coriander, leaves picked

6 radishes

1 tablespoon sesame seeds

4 spring onions, cut into batons

½ lime

Sesame spiced dressing

½ heaped teaspoon English mustard

2 teaspoons sugar

1 clove garlic, crushed

2½ tablespoons smooth peanut butter

½ tablespoon tahini

2 tablespoons toasted sesame seeds

2 teaspoons hot chilli sauce

3 tablespoons sour cream

2 tablespoons mayonnaise

1½ teaspoons sea salt flakes

juice of 1 lemon

50 ml water

SLOW-ROASTED PORK BELLY WITH CUCUMBER, CORIANDER AND SESAME-SPICED DRESSING

You will only need about half of the pork for this dish, but there are many ways to enjoy the leftovers. One of my favourites is a sandwich made with crusty bread, thin slices of cold roast pork, crisp apple, coriander, red or green chilli and a splash of fish sauce. Divine! Always buy organic for a sweeter, more delicate flavour.

Preheat oven to 140°C (fan-forced).

Score the skin of the belly and then rub all over with the oil and salt flakes. Place on a rack in a roasting tin. Pour the water into the tin and roast on the middle shelf of the oven for 2½ hours, basting regularly. The meat should be wonderfully tender and the skin should be crispy and crackly.

Allow the pork to cool to room temperature, then slice half the meat as thinly as possible – it will shatter as you do so, but I think this adds a lovely rustic appeal to the salad.

To make the dressing, blend all the ingredients with a stick blender until smooth. Transfer to a serving jug.

Arrange the pork slices on a platter. Pile the cucumber slices around the edge, topped with the coriander leaves, radishes, sesame seeds and spring onion batons. Squeeze over a little lime juice and sprinkle over a little extra salt. Serve the dressing separately so your guests can add as much or as little as they like, or just drizzle it over at the last minute.

THE GREEK FEAST

DOMATOKEFTEDES

YOGHURT, GREEN CHILLI AND MINT DIP
WITH FRIED BEANS AND PAPRIKA

SWEET AND SOUR DRIED FIGS
ON PAN-FRIED HALOUMI

ROLLED SARDINE FILLETS BAKED
WITH VINE LEAVES AND TOMATO

BARBECUED OCTOPUS

SLOW-BAKED LAMB SHOULDER

FREEKAH SALAD WITH FETA, TOASTED
ALMONDS, LEMON AND PARSLEY

MAROULI SALAD

SLOW-COOKED ZUCCHINI WITH TOMATO,
LEMON AND CORIANDER DRESSING

CHOCOLATE MOUSSE WITH COFFEE GRANITA

ALMOND AND CLOVE BAKLAVA WITH CITRUS SYRUP

170 g semi-dried tomatoes, roughly chopped

1 tablespoon extra virgin olive oil

1 small brown onion, finely diced

3 cloves garlic, finely chopped

8 ripe tomatoes, blanched, peeled, seeded and diced
  (you need about 350 g)

¼ bunch flat-leaf parsley, leaves picked and finely chopped

¼ bunch mint, leaves picked and finely chopped

1 tablespoon dried oregano

½ bunch spring onions, finely sliced

sea salt and freshly ground black pepper

175 g plain flour

1 tablespoon baking powder

vegetable oil, for deep-frying

lemon wedges, to serve

plain yoghurt, to serve

fennel fronds and mint leaves, to serve (optional)

DOMATOKEFTEDES

These tasty little tomato fritters are traditionally eaten during Lent.

Place the semi-dried tomatoes in a small bowl and cover with boiling water. Soak for 20 minutes, then drain well.

Heat the olive oil in a small saucepan over medium heat and cook the onion and garlic for 2–3 minutes or until the onion is golden.

Place the semi-dried tomatoes, onion and garlic mixture, diced tomato, herbs and spring onion in a large bowl. Stir well and season with salt and pepper. Combine the flour and baking powder, then add to the tomato mixture and stir well to combine. Allow to rest for 15 minutes.

Pour vegetable oil into a deep frying pan to a depth of 8 cm and heat over medium heat to 170°C or until a cube of bread browns in 20 seconds. Add tablespoons of the fritter mixture and cook for 2 minutes. Turn the fritters over, flatten slightly with the back of a spoon and cook for another 1–2 minutes. Remove from the pan and drain on paper towel. Cover and keep warm while you make the remaining fritters.

Serve with lemon wedges, a sprinkle of sea salt and a dollop of yoghurt. Garnish with fennel fronds and mint leaves, if using.

500 g thick Greek-style yoghurt

2 green chillies, chopped

½ bunch mint, leaves picked and finely chopped

juice of ½ lemon

sea salt and freshly ground black pepper

4 tablespoons extra virgin olive oil

400 g can butter beans, drained and rinsed

3 cloves garlic, sliced

2 teaspoons smoked sweet paprika

200 g dried figs

120 ml red wine or sherry vinegar

120 g brown sugar

1 tablespoon black peppercorns, crushed

1 small red chilli, split

1 clove garlic, sliced

1 bay leaf

4–5 thyme sprigs

200 ml water

2 pinches of salt

4 tablespoons extra virgin olive oil

250 g haloumi, cut lengthways into thick slices

YOGHURT, GREEN CHILLI AND MINT DIP WITH FRIED BEANS AND PAPRIKA

This sauce-style dip goes with meat or fish, or serve it on its own with bread.

Combine the yoghurt, chilli, mint and lemon juice in a medium bowl. Season with salt and pepper and stir in half the olive oil.

Heat the remaining olive oil in a large frying pan over medium heat and cook the butter beans for a few minutes or until the skins start to split. Season with salt, then add the garlic and cook for 2–3 minutes or until golden. Stir in the paprika and remove from the heat.

Transfer the yoghurt mixture to a serving dish and spoon over the beans.

Pictured page 186.

SWEET AND SOUR DRIED FIGS ON PAN-FRIED HALOUMI

This unusual dish is great with drinks or as a starter. The salty fried cheese is the perfect flavour base.

Place the figs in a bowl, cover with boiling water and soak for 1 hour. Drain and set aside.

Combine the vinegar, sugar, peppercorns, chilli, garlic, bay leaf, thyme sprigs, water and salt in a medium saucepan and simmer over low heat for 2 minutes. Add the figs and cook for a further 5 minutes. Remove the pan from the heat and allow the flavours to infuse.

Heat a large frying pan over high heat for 2 minutes, then add the olive oil and reduce the heat to medium. Fry the cheese slices for a few minutes each side until golden brown.

Arrange the haloumi on a serving plate. Slice the figs through the middle and place on top of the cheese. Drizzle with the fig syrup and serve immediately.

Pictured page 187.

SERVES 4–6

160 ml extra virgin olive oil

2 red onions, sliced

3 cloves garlic, sliced

15 large semi-dried tomatoes

28 fresh sardine fillets

sea salt and freshly ground black pepper

3 vine leaves, lightly rinsed and finely shredded

3 cloves garlic, extra, diced

5 sprigs oregano, leaves picked

200 ml tomato sugo (Italian tomato sauce)

4 tablespoons white wine

1 handful fine fresh breadcrumbs

2 vine leaves, extra

ROLLED SARDINE FILLETS BAKED WITH VINE LEAVES AND TOMATO

These are delicious served hot from the oven but are also lovely at room temperature. Look for the freshest sardine fillets available – they should be pink.

Preheat the oven to 200°C (fan-forced).

Heat half the olive oil in a frying pan over medium heat and cook the onion and garlic for 30 minutes or until the onion is soft and caramelised.

Meanwhile, place the semi-dried tomatoes in a small saucepan and cover with hot water. Simmer over low heat for 5 minutes, then drain, reserving the liquid. Roughly chop the tomatoes.

Place the sardine fillets on a flat surface, skin-side down, and season with salt and pepper. Spread a little caramelised onion on each, then divide the shredded vine leaves, semi-dried tomatoes, garlic and oregano among the fillets. Roll them up from head end to tail.

Spread 2 tablespoons tomato sugo and 1 tablespoon olive oil in the bottom of a baking dish large enough to fit the rolled sardines in a single layer. Tightly pack the sardines in the dish and season with salt and pepper, then pour over the wine, reserved tomato liquid, remaining olive oil and remaining sugo. Sprinkle with breadcrumbs and place the extra vine leaves on top.

Bake for about 30 minutes or until hot and bubbling. Serve warm or hot.

Yoghurt, green chilli and mint dip with
fried beans and paprika (see page 184)

Sweet and sour dried figs on pan-fried
haloumi (see page 184)

6 sprigs oregano, leaves picked and chopped

2 tablespoons dried oregano

4 cloves garlic, smashed

120 ml white or red wine vinegar

100 ml vegetable oil

1.5 kg octopus legs, cleaned (ask your fishmonger
    to do this)

1 tablespoon extra virgin olive oil, plus extra for drizzling

100 g good-quality Greek feta

extra sprigs oregano, to serve (optional)

lemon wedges, to serve

BARBECUED OCTOPUS

The secret to tender octopus lies in marinating then
braising it before barbecuing.

Combine the fresh and dried oregano, garlic, vinegar
and vegetable oil in a large glass or stainless-steel bowl.
Add the octopus, then cover with plastic film and
marinate in the fridge for about 2 hours.

Transfer the octopus and its marinade to a large
saucepan and bring to the boil over medium heat,
then reduce the heat and simmer for 15 minutes.
Remove the octopus from the pan and lightly brush
with extra virgin olive oil.

Preheat a chargrill or barbecue plate to hot. Cook
the octopus for 1–2 minutes each side. Serve with
the feta, oregano sprigs (if using) and lemon wedges,
drizzled with a little extra olive oil.

2 tablespoons sea salt flakes

8 cloves garlic, sliced

6 sprigs rosemary, stripped and leaves chopped

1 tablespoon black peppercorns

100 ml extra virgin olive oil

3 tablespoons dried oregano

1.8–2.2 kg lamb shoulder, boned

100 ml white wine vinegar

lemon wedges, to serve (optional)

flatbread, to serve (optional)

300 g freekah grain

2 handfuls large golden raisins

100 ml extra virgin olive oil

juice of 1 lemon

sea salt and freshly ground black pepper

1 red onion, finely diced

1 large bunch flat-leaf parsley, leaves picked
   and roughly chopped

50 g almonds, toasted and roughly chopped

100 g marinated sheep's feta, crumbled

SLOW-BAKED LAMB SHOULDER

This lamb is to die for! You will find yourself cooking
it again and again – as I do.

Preheat the oven to 150°C (fan-forced).

Grind the salt, garlic, rosemary and peppercorns in
a mortar and pestle, then add the olive oil and dried
oregano.

Open out the lamb shoulder and massage the marinade
into the lamb. Place the lamb in a ceramic baking dish,
splash over the vinegar and pour 150 ml water into the
tray. Cover with foil and bake for 2½ hours. Remove
the foil (the meat should be very tender by now) and
drain off some of the fat, leaving the juices behind.

Increase the heat to 220°C (200°C fan-forced) and
turn on the grill bars if possible, then cook the meat
for 3–5 minutes until crispy and nicely browned.

Lightly shred the meat into large chunks and pile on
a warm platter (or serve it in the baking dish – try to
keep it as hot as possible). Spoon over some of the juices
and serve with lemon wedges and flatbread, if liked.

FREEKAH SALAD WITH FETA, TOASTED ALMONDS, LEMON AND PARSLEY

This salad is particularly good served with the
slow-baked lamb shoulder (left) and the yoghurt dip
(see page 184). Freekah is a nutty, cracked green
wheat, available from health-food shops. If you can't
find it, pearl barley is the perfect substitute.

Bring a large saucepan of water to the boil over high
heat. Add the freekah, then reduce the heat to low and
simmer for 40 minutes or until tender.

Meanwhile, soak the raisins in boiling water for a few
minutes to plump them up. Drain.

Drain the freekah well and place in a serving bowl.
Add the olive oil, lemon juice, salt and pepper to
the warm freekah, then toss through the onion and
parsley. Top with the toasted almonds and feta.

Slow-baked lamb shoulder (see page 192)

Marouli salad (see page 196)

2 cos lettuces, cut into 2 cm slices

3 Lebanese (small) cucumbers, cut into quarters
    lengthways

¼ bunch dill, leaves picked and chopped

¼ bunch flat-leaf parsley, leaves picked
    and finely chopped

½ bunch spring onions, finely chopped

Feta and lemon dressing

125 g Greek-style yoghurt

80 g good-quality Greek feta (such as Dodoni brand)

juice of 1 lemon

4 tablespoons extra virgin olive oil

3 teaspoons sugar

freshly ground black pepper

15 small zucchini (courgettes), washed,
    trimmed and cut into thick rounds

200 ml water

100 ml extra virgin olive oil

2 fresh bay leaves

sea salt and freshly ground black pepper

Tomato, lemon and coriander dressing

2 cloves garlic, sliced

2 teaspoons sea salt

3 tablespoons coriander seeds, toasted

100 ml extra virgin olive oil

6 ripe tomatoes, finely diced

¼ bunch flat-leaf parsley, leaves picked
    and finely shredded

½ bunch coriander, leaves picked and finely shredded

1 teaspoon freshly ground black pepper

juice of 1 lemon

MAROULI SALAD

This cos salad epitomises uncomplicated Greek cooking. The light, fresh flavours are a great match for the lamb and rolled sardine fillets. Try them also with barbounia.

To make the dressing, place the yoghurt, feta and lemon juice in a medium bowl and blend with a stick blender until smooth. Add the olive oil and sugar and blend until combined. Season with pepper.

Place the lettuce and cucumber in a bowl. Scatter the herbs and spring onion over the top, then drizzle with the dressing.

Pictured page 195.

SLOW-COOKED ZUCCHINI WITH TOMATO, LEMON AND CORIANDER DRESSING

The zucchini takes on a mellow flavour that works beautifully with the vibrant dressing.

Preheat the oven to 180°C (fan-forced).

Place the zucchini, water, olive oil, bay leaves, salt and pepper in a large ovenproof dish with a tight-fitting lid. Bake for 45 minutes or until well softened. Remove from the oven and set aside.

To make the dressing, grind the garlic, salt and coriander seeds to a rough paste in a mortar and pestle. Stir in the olive oil, then transfer the mixture to a bowl. Add the tomato, parsley and coriander, then season with pepper. Just before serving, stir in the lemon juice.

Serve straight from the baking dish if you like, or transfer the zucchini to a shallow serving dish and spoon the dressing over the top.

SERVES 10

thick cream, to serve

Coffee granita

380 ml hot espresso coffee

90 g caster sugar

1 tablespoon liquid glucose

Chocolate mousse

300 g dark couverture chocolate, chopped

150 g unsalted butter, at room temperature

6 eggs, separated

2½ tablespoons white rum

40 g caster sugar

250 ml pouring cream, lightly whipped

Swirls

200 g dark chocolate buttons

10 coffee beans

CHOCOLATE MOUSSE WITH COFFEE GRANITA

I love the texture of this dessert – the clash of fudgy mousse and icy granita. Use freshly made espresso and the best dark chocolate you can afford. It really does make a difference.

To make the granita, stir all the ingredients in a bowl until the sugar has dissolved. Pour the mixture into a plastic container and freeze for 4 hours. When frozen, scratch the surface with a fork to make granita flakes.

For the mousse, melt the chocolate in a large heatproof bowl over a saucepan of barely simmering water (don't let the bowl touch the water), then stir in the butter, egg yolks and rum until smooth. Whisk the egg whites and sugar until soft peaks form and fold through the chocolate mixture. Fold in the cream and stir gently until smooth. Cover and refrigerate.

To make the swirls, line a baking tray with baking paper and melt the chocolate in a bowl as above. Set aside until the chocolate cools and thickens slightly. If you don't have a piping bag, make one by folding a large triangle of baking paper into a cone, folding the top edges inside. Pour the chocolate into the cone and cut the tip off to about the size of a ballpoint pen nib. Pipe 10 chocolate spirals onto the prepared baking tray and place a coffee bean in the centre of each. Set aside to cool to room temperature for 1 hour, then place in the fridge for 15 minutes or until firm. Remove carefully with a spatula.

To serve, scoop the mousse into 10 chilled glasses. Top each with granita and a dollop of cream, and finish with a chocolate swirl.

SERVES 10–12

280 g almonds, toasted

180 g brown sugar

2 teaspoons ground cloves

1 teaspoon ground cinnamon

8 seeded prunes, finely diced

560 g filo pastry (about 1½ packets)

250 g unsalted butter, melted

cloves, for decorating

Citrus syrup

grated zest and juice of 2 lemons

grated zest and juice of 1 orange

300 g caster sugar

100 g honey

2 cloves

2 cinnamon sticks

200 ml water

ALMOND AND CLOVE BAKLAVA WITH CITRUS SYRUP

These sweet delights are loosely based on traditional baklava but are not quite as sweet and have a lovely citrus tang – perfect for that little sugar pick-me-up at the end of a party.

Preheat the oven to 160°C (fan-forced). Brush the base of a 40 cm round baking dish with butter.

To make the citrus syrup, combine all the ingredients in a small saucepan over medium heat and stir for about 10 minutes until the sugar has dissolved. Remove the pan from the heat and set aside to cool at room temperature.

Place the nuts, sugar, ground cloves and cinnamon in a food processor and process until the nuts are coarsely chopped. Transfer to a bowl and stir in the prunes.

Place one sheet of filo pastry in the baking dish, brush with butter then place another sheet on top. Repeat with another six sheets, brushing with butter between each layer. Sprinkle about 5 tablespoons of the nut mixture on top. Lay two sheets of filo over the nuts and brush with butter, then sprinkle on more nut mix. Repeat until you have used all the nut mix, then finish with another six layers of buttered filo.

Score the top in a diamond fashion and stick a clove in the centre of each diamond. Roll the overhanging pastry into the edge to form a rim, then brush with butter.

Bake for 22–30 minutes or until golden. Allow to cool slightly and then drench evenly with the warm syrup. For best results, allow to rest for 2 hours before cutting into diamonds and serving. The baklava will keep for 4 days in an airtight container (if they last that long).

COMFORT FOOD DINNER

HAM HOCK, RED LENTIL AND TOMATO BROTH

BEETROOT SLAW WITH APPLE
AND RED CABBAGE

ROAST CHICKEN WITH SHREDDED
SPINACH AND YOGHURT

YOGHURT, HONEY AND CHOCOLATE CAKE

SERVES 6–8

1 large ham hock (700–900 g)

2 litres water

2 litres chicken stock

4 tablespoons extra virgin olive oil

2 brown onions, diced

1 leek, sliced

5 cloves garlic, sliced

2 sticks celery, sliced

1 carrot, peeled and sliced

1 bay leaf

4 sprigs thyme

1 cinnamon stick

2 teaspoons fennel seeds

1 tablespoon cumin seeds, roughly ground

1 red chilli, sliced

1 tablespoon tomato paste (puree)

400 g can crushed tomatoes

½ cup (100 g) brown rice

1 cup (200 g) red lentils

250 g plain yoghurt

hot chilli sauce, to taste

¼ bunch coriander, leaves picked

mountain bread or other light flatbread,
   to serve (optional)

HAM HOCK, RED LENTIL AND TOMATO BROTH

I really recommend using an organic ham hock for this (or you could use the knuckle end of a leftover ham). Ask your butcher to cut it into pieces to make it easier to handle.

Place the ham hock, water and half the chicken stock in a very large saucepan. Bring to the boil, then reduce the heat to low and simmer, partially covered, for 20 minutes.

Heat the olive oil in a saucepan over medium heat and cook the onion, leek, garlic, celery and carrot for 10 minutes or until golden. Stir in the herbs and spices.

Add the cooked vegetables to the hock mixture, along with the tomato paste, crushed tomatoes, rice, lentils and remaining stock. Simmer over low heat for about an hour until the soup is thick and flavoursome. If you think the soup is getting a little too thick during cooking, add some more water. Taste and adjust the seasoning if necessary.

Spoon in a little yoghurt, drizzle with the chilli sauce and finish with a sprinkling of coriander. Serve with mountain bread (if using).

SERVES 4–6

2 beetroot, peeled and cut into matchsticks
½ red onion, chopped
¼ red cabbage, shaved thinly
50 g walnuts, roughly chopped and toasted
1 granny smith apple, cored and cut into matchsticks
4 sprigs mint, leaves picked
extra virgin olive oil, for coating
sea salt and freshly ground black pepper

Dressing
3 heaped tablespoons sour cream
4 tablespoons extra virgin olive oil
juice of 1 large lemon
2 tablespoons raw sugar
1½ tablespoons red wine vinegar
sea salt and freshly ground black pepper

BEETROOT SLAW WITH APPLE AND RED CABBAGE

This is a great alternative to traditional coleslaw.
It goes really well with the roast chicken, roast pork
or simply enjoy it on its own.

Combine the beetroot, onion and cabbage in a bowl.

To make the dressing, whisk together all the ingredients
in a small bowl until smooth. Pour the dressing over
the salad and scrunch with your hands to combine well.

Toss the walnuts, apple and mint in a little olive oil and
season with salt and pepper.

Place the cabbage in a serving bowl and top with the
apple and walnut mixture.

100 g bulgur (cracked wheat)

½ teaspoon ras el hanout

250 ml boiling water

5 tablespoons plain yoghurt

3 tablespoons extra virgin olive oil

½ red onion, finely chopped

1 tablespoon red wine vinegar

1 handful small basil leaves, shredded

1 handful sorrel leaves, shredded (optional)

2 large handfuls baby spinach leaves, shredded

50 g pine nuts, toasted

sea salt and freshly ground black pepper

½ bought roast free-range chicken, bones removed,
   cut into bite-sized pieces

2 small red chillies, finely sliced

½ lemon

ROAST CHICKEN WITH SHREDDED SPINACH AND YOGHURT

Roast free-range chickens are becoming more widely available. If you keep asking your local chicken shop or supermarket to stock free-range chooks, eventually they will.

Place the bulgur in a saucepan, add the ras el hanout and boiling water and simmer over low heat for 4–5 minutes. Drain.

Combine the yoghurt, olive oil, onion and vinegar in a large bowl. Set half aside for later. Stir in the bulgur, basil, sorrel (if using), spinach and half the pine nuts, and season with salt and pepper. Add the chicken pieces and toss gently to combine.

To serve, spoon the reserved yoghurt mixture over the top and scatter over the chilli and remaining pine nuts. Finish with a good squeeze of lemon juice.

130 g plain flour

130 g self-raising flour

1 teaspoon baking powder

½ teaspoon pouring salt

2 eggs

140 g honey, plus extra for drizzling (optional)

280 g butter, melted

170 g plain yoghurt

110 g raw sugar

150 g good-quality dark chocolate buttons

1 vanilla bean, finely sliced on the diagonal

YOGHURT, HONEY AND CHOCOLATE CAKE

This cake is rich and buttery and very easy to make. For me, a tiny piece makes the perfect afternoon pick-me-up. Use couverture chocolate for the best results.

Preheat the oven to 180°C (fan-forced). Grease and line a 22 cm square cake tin with baking paper.

Sift the flours, baking powder and salt into a bowl. Beat the eggs in a separate bowl until light and fluffy, then add the honey, butter, yoghurt and sugar. Whisk together well, then gently fold in the flour mixture and chocolate buttons.

Pour the mixture into the tin and sprinkle the vanilla bean over the top. Bake for 40 minutes or until a skewer inserted into the centre comes out clean. Cool in the tin for 5 minutes, then turn out onto a wire rack to cool completely. Serve drizzled with a little extra honey, if liked.

WELLBEING MENU

SOBA NOODLE SALAD WITH BROCCOLI,
CHICKEN AND TOASTED NORI

AVOCADO WITH SPROUTS AND
UMEBOSHI PLUM DRESSING

CALAMARI AND BULGUR SALAD WITH
MINT, CHILLI AND ASPARAGUS

SESAME BEEF WITH SPRING ONIONS,
GREEN CHILLI AND BROWN RICE

FREE-FORM PEACH TART

SERVES 8

300 g soba noodles

1 head broccoli, cut into florets

2 tablespoons sesame seeds

2 teaspoons sesame oil

100 ml ponzu

4 tablespoons extra virgin olive oil

6 cm piece ginger, finely diced

½ roast free-range chicken,
   meat removed and torn

5 spring onions, finely sliced

1 sheet toasted nori, shredded

SERVES 2

3 perfectly ripe avocados, carefully diced

4 spring onions, finely sliced

100 g snow pea shoots

60 g chickpea sprouts

50 g mung bean sprouts

50 g lentil sprouts

sesame seeds, for sprinkling

Umeboshi plum dressing

2 tablespoons umeboshi plum puree

2 tablespoons rice vinegar

3 tablespoons extra virgin olive oil

juice of ½ lemon

½ teaspoon sesame oil

¼ clove garlic, finely diced

pinch of sea salt flakes

< SOBA NOODLE SALAD WITH BROCCOLI, CHICKEN AND TOASTED NORI

This Asian-style salad is dead easy to make, super-tasty and good for you. It also holds really well, which means you can make it a bit in advance. Green tea is the perfect accompaniment. Ponzu and toasted nori sheets are available from Asian food stores and some large supermarkets.

Cook the noodles in a small saucepan of boiling water for 3 minutes. Drain and refresh under cold water. Drain again.

Cook the broccoli in a saucepan of lightly salted boiling water for 2 minutes. Drain.

Combine the sesame seeds, sesame oil, ponzu, olive oil and ginger in a large bowl. Add the noodles, broccoli, chicken and spring onion and toss to combine. Serve sprinkled with nori.

AVOCADO WITH SPROUTS AND UMEBOSHI PLUM DRESSING

This is a super-food salad that is full of goodness. Umeboshi plum puree is great for easing cold and flu symptoms, and its sharp lemon flavour is just divine with the sprouts and avocado. You'll find it in Asian supermarkets and health-food stores.

To make the dressing, combine all the ingredients in a small bowl.

Arrange the avocado on a platter, then scatter the spring onion, shoots, sprouts and sesame seeds over the top. Spoon over the dressing and serve.

Pictured page 216.

½ cup (80 g) fine bulgur (cracked wheat)

1 clove garlic, peeled

3 teaspoons dried chilli flakes

2 long red chillies

sea salt, to taste

2 teaspoons black peppercorns

finely grated zest and juice of 2 lemons

150 ml extra virgin olive oil, plus extra for brushing

¼ bunch mint, leaves picked and coarsely chopped

¼ bunch flat-leaf parsley, leaves picked and
   coarsely chopped

3 calamari hoods, cleaned with flaps attached,
   legs reserved

freshly ground black pepper

½ red onion, finely sliced

1 bunch asparagus, trimmed

sliced red chilli, extra, to garnish

lemon halves, to serve

CALAMARI AND BULGUR SALAD WITH MINT, CHILLI AND ASPARAGUS

This may seem like an unusual combination but it will be a dish you will want to make again and again.

Soak the bulgur in enough boiling water to just cover for 15 minutes. Drain if necessary.

Grind the garlic, dried and fresh chilli, sea salt and black peppercorns in a mortar and pestle until a coarse paste forms. Add the lemon zest, a third of the olive oil, and half the mint and parsley and grind to a green paste, adding a little more oil if necessary.

Preheat a chargrill or barbecue plate to medium. Halve the calamari lengthways and thread diagonally onto long metal skewers, adding the legs at the ends. Drizzle with half the remaining olive oil and season with salt and pepper. Cook the calamari skewers for about 5–8 minutes or until just cooked. Remove the skewers and slice the calamari into strips, then stir through the paste while still hot.

Combine the bulgur and lemon juice in a large bowl with the remaining olive oil. Add the red onion and season to taste, then add the calamari.

Brush the asparagus with a little extra olive oil and grill for 3 minutes. Lay them on a platter and top with the bulgur mixture and warm dressed calamari. Sprinkle over the remaining mint and parsley and the extra chilli, squeeze over some lemon juice and serve.

SERVES 2

1 large handful wakame seaweed

2 teaspoons sesame oil

1¼ tablespoons light soy sauce

100 ml Shaoxing rice wine

2½ tablespoons oyster sauce

2 teaspoons sugar

4 tablespoons peanut or vegetable oil

½ brown onion, sliced into half moons

5 cm piece ginger, cut into matchsticks

2 cloves garlic, sliced

300 g eye fillet steak, thinly sliced

3 tablespoons sesame seeds

4 shiitake mushrooms, sliced

4 spring onions, sliced diagonally

1 large green chilli, thinly sliced

1½ cups (300 g) brown rice, cooked

100 g pea shoots, trimmed

250 g bean sprouts

½ bunch coriander, leaves picked

SESAME BEEF WITH SPRING ONIONS, GREEN CHILLI AND BROWN RICE

This dish is also wonderful with chicken or firm tofu instead of beef. Whatever you choose, the result will be wonderfully tasty.

Boil the wakame in a saucepan of boiling water for 15 minutes or until tender. Drain and thinly slice.

Meanwhile, combine the sesame oil, soy sauce, rice wine, oyster sauce and sugar in a bowl and set aside.

Heat 2½ tablespoons oil in a large wok over high heat. When the oil is hot and shimmering, add the onion, ginger and garlic and stir-fry for 30 seconds. Add the steak and sesame seeds and cook for 1 minute, stirring occasionally, then remove from the wok.

Heat the remaining oil in the wok and cook the mushrooms, spring onion and chilli for 1 minute. Return the steak to the wok, add the soy sauce mixture, rice, pea shoots, bean sprouts and wakame and stir-fry for 1 minute. Scatter the coriander over the top and serve immediately.

SERVES 8

300 g butter
150 g icing sugar
2 eggs
600 g plain flour
10 ripe peaches, each cut into 6 wedges
150 g raw sugar, plus 2 tablespoons extra for sprinkling
½ nutmeg, grated (or 1 teaspoon ground nutmeg)
finely grated zest of ½ lemon

FREE-FORM PEACH TART

This rustic-looking tart is irresistible with a scoop
of ice-cream or a dollop of cream. You can use
nectarines in place of peaches if you like.

Preheat the oven to 190°C (fan-forced).

Place the butter, icing sugar and eggs in a food
processor and pulse until combined. Add the flour and
process until the mixture comes together. Turn out the
dough onto a floured surface and gently press together,
then wrap in plastic film and rest in the fridge for
20 minutes.

Combine the peach, sugar, nutmeg and lemon zest
in a bowl, toss gently and set aside for 15 minutes.

Roll out the pastry on a large sheet of baking paper to
a thickness of about 3 cm. Lift the baking paper and
pastry onto a large baking tray and trim the edges so
the pastry is a rough oval or circle.

Pile the fruit in the centre of the pastry and use the
baking paper to lift the sides over so the pastry half-covers
the fruit, leaving an opening in the centre. Sprinkle with
the extra sugar and bake for 45–55 minutes or until
cooked and golden. Brush the pastry with any juices
before serving.

BIG BRUNCH

PINEAPPLE TOSSED IN SHREDDED COCONUT
WITH MANGO AND BLUEBERRIES

GINGER LEMONADE WITH ANGOSTURA BITTERS

RICOTTA TARTS WITH CURED OCEAN TROUT

HAM AND POTATO FRITTATA WITH WITLOF RELISH

TOASTED BIRCHER-STYLE MUESLI

EGG AND SILVERBEET WRAP WITH FETA AND DUKKAH

MOROCCAN SEMOLINA PANCAKES
WITH HONEYCOMB BUTTER

CHARGRILLED ASPARAGUS WITH CHERRY
TOMATOES AND BUFFALO MOZZARELLA

SOUR-CREAM PASTRY TART WITH
SMOKED TROUT AND CARAMELISED ONION

GREEN EGG AND PANCETTA PUFF-PASTRY PIE

SCRAMBLED EGGS WITH
CHORIZO AND SPRING ONIONS

RICOTTA ON TOAST WITH FIGS AND HONEY

CHOCOLATE AND BEETROOT BROWNIES

CHOCOLATE AND BANANA LOAF

BAKED BEANS WITH MUSTARD
SEEDS, VINEGAR AND TOMATO

SERVES 6–8

1 large ripe pineapple, skin removed
1½ cups (115 g) shredded coconut
2 ripe mangoes, cut in cheeks, halved and scored
1 punnet (150 g) blueberries

MAKES ABOUT 750 ML

400 g raw sugar
100 ml water
finely grated zest and juice of 10 lemons
4 cm piece ginger, grated

Ice cubes
Angostura bitters
24 lemon blossoms (optional)

< PINEAPPLE TOSSED IN SHREDDED COCONUT WITH MANGO AND BLUEBERRIES

There is something about pineapple and shredded coconut that just works really well. This is a very simple dish to make but the complexity of flavours makes it taste like something special.

Cut the pineapple in half lengthways, then cut in long lengths along the core into long wedges. Toss in the coconut until well coated.

Lay the pineapple wedges out flat on a platter and top with the flexed mango cheeks. Scatter with blueberries and serve.

GINGER LEMONADE WITH ANGOSTURA BITTERS

This is so refreshing on a hot day. The infused cordial-style syrup will keep for a few weeks in the fridge undiluted.

For the ice cubes, add 2 drops of Angostura bitters and a lemon blossom (if using) into 24 ice-cube holes. Fill with water and freeze.

Combine the sugar and water in a saucepan over medium heat and stir until the sugar has dissolved. Simmer for 3 minutes, then add the lemon zest and ginger and boil for 1 minute. Set aside to cool for 10 minutes, then stir in the lemon juice. Strain into a bottle and refrigerate.

To serve, combine 1 part cordial to 3 parts water and pour over the ice cubes.

Pictured pages 234–235.

8 sheets filo pastry

80 g butter, melted

150 g fresh ricotta, well drained

1 tablespoon dukkah (see page 114), plus extra to serve

sea salt and freshly ground black pepper

24 slices cured ocean trout

1 tablespoon caperberries

juice of 1 lemon

½ red onion, finely chopped

lemon wedges, to serve

RICOTTA TARTS WITH CURED OCEAN TROUT

These tarts are deliciously decadent. Admittedly, the pastry is a little fiddly but the results are worth it. Just thank your lucky stars you don't have to make the filo.

Preheat the oven to 200°C (fan-forced). Line a baking tray with baking paper.

Place one sheet of filo on a flat surface and brush generously with butter. Place another sheet on top, overlapping the first to make a rectangle about 35 cm × 40 cm. Place a third and fourth filo sheet on top in the same way, brushing with butter in between. Use the remaining four sheets of filo to make a second tart base.

Cut each pastry rectangle lengthways into three equal strips. Place 1 tablespoon ricotta in the middle of a strip and spread it out to form a round shape. Beginning with an edge close to the ricotta, twist and roll the pastry inwards, moving around as you go, to form a little tart. Brush with butter, sprinkle with dukkah and season with salt and pepper. Repeat to make another five tarts.

Place the tarts on the baking tray and bake for about 10–15 minutes or until golden. Remove and allow to cool for a few minutes. Top each one with two slices of ocean trout, caperberries, lemon juice and a little red onion. Serve with lemon wedges and extra dukkah.

4 tablespoons extra virgin olive oil

2 cloves garlic, finely chopped

1 potato, cooked and crushed

150 g ham off the bone, chopped

4 sprigs oregano, leaves picked

6 eggs

100 ml pouring cream

sea salt and freshly ground black pepper

80 g grated parmesan

2 handfuls flat-leaf parsley, leaves picked

fresh bread rolls, to serve

Witlof relish

2 tablespoons extra virgin olive oil

3 sprigs thyme, leaves picked

2 red onions, halved and thinly sliced

1 teaspoon sea salt

5 witlof (chicory), finely sliced

100 g brown sugar

4 tablespoons red wine vinegar

freshly ground black pepper

HAM AND POTATO FRITTATA WITH WITLOF RELISH

Much as I love good ham off the bone, there are only so many toasted ham sandwiches you can eat – so here's another way to enjoy it. Leftover relish will keep for a week in the fridge or you can use your favourite chutney instead.

To make the witlof relish, heat the olive oil in a large saucepan over low heat. Add the thyme, onion and salt and cook, stirring occasionally, for 5 minutes. Add the witlof and cook, stirring occasionally, for 10 minutes. Stir in the sugar and cook over medium heat for about 3–4 minutes until caramelised. Add the vinegar and pepper, increase the heat to high and cook for about 2 minutes, stirring occasionally. Remove from the heat and allow to cool to room temperature. This makes about 2 cups (640 g).

Preheat the oven to 160°C (fan-forced).

Heat 1 tablespoon olive oil in a small frying pan over medium heat and cook the garlic for 2–3 minutes or until aromatic. Stir in the potato, ham and oregano and cook for 4–5 minutes until crispy and golden.

Place the eggs and cream in a bowl and beat lightly with a fork. Season with salt and pepper, then stir in the ham and potato mixture, parmesan and parsley.

Heat the remaining olive oil in a medium non-stick frying pan with an ovenproof handle over medium heat. Pour in the egg mixture, stir a few times, then transfer to the oven and bake for 20–25 minutes until set and golden on top.

Cool slightly, then cut into wedges and serve with the witlof relish in bread rolls.

SERVES 8

250 g plain yoghurt

2 cups (260 g) toasted muesli

160 ml apple juice or water

juice of 1 lemon

½ teaspoon ground cinnamon

1½ handfuls hazelnuts, toasted, plus extra to garnish

2 granny smith apples, cut into matchsticks

200 g plain yoghurt, extra

2 tablespoons honey

< TOASTED BIRCHER-STYLE MUESLI

This is my version of bircher muesli and I love it.
I use toasted muesli, rather than soaking it for hours,
which makes it really quick and really yummy.

In a medium bowl, combine the yoghurt, muesli,
apple juice or water, lemon juice and cinnamon.

Place the hazelnuts and apple in a bowl and mix well.

Divide the muesli among small bowls and spoon the
apple mixture on top. Finish with a dollop of extra
yoghurt, a scattering of extra hazelnuts and a final
drizzle of honey.

SERVES 2

1½ tablespoons olive oil

1 large clove garlic, finely sliced

sea salt and freshly ground black pepper

15 leaves silverbeet (Swiss chard),
    stems trimmed and finely shredded

1 large egg

40 g feta

1 piece Lebanese bread

¼ lemon

2 tablespoons dukkah (see page 114)

½ green chilli, finely sliced

EGG AND SILVERBEET WRAP WITH FETA AND DUKKAH

I am addicted to silverbeet at the moment – the leaves
and stems are equally delicious. Make as many of these
as you need, wrap them in baking paper and enjoy them
in the sunshine.

Heat 1 tablespoon olive oil in a medium non-stick
frying pan over medium heat for 1 minute. Add the
garlic, salt, pepper and silverbeet and cook, stirring
frequently, for about 5–6 minutes or until the silverbeet
is wilted.

Make a space in the middle of the silverbeet, add the
remaining olive oil and crack the egg into the oil.
Season and crumble the feta over the egg and silverbeet.
Cook for about 4 minutes or until the egg is cooked
to your liking, then place in the centre of the bread.

Squeeze the lemon over the silverbeet and scatter with
the dukkah and green chilli. Roll up tightly and cut in
half to serve.

100 g honeycomb (see page 164),
  smashed to a rough dust

150 g unsalted butter, softened

210 ml warm water

2 teaspoons dried yeast

1 large egg

120 ml milk

1 cup (160 g) fine semolina

1 cup (150 g) plain flour

2 tablespoons raw sugar

80 g butter, extra for pan-frying

4 ripe ladyfinger bananas, peeled
  and sliced on an angle

4 tablespoons honey

lemon juice, to serve (optional)

icing sugar, for dusting (optional)

MOROCCAN SEMOLINA PANCAKES WITH HONEYCOMB BUTTER AND BANANA

The semolina in this recipe gives a lovely chewiness to the pancakes.

Combine the honeycomb and butter in a bowl and set aside.

Combine the warm water and yeast in a medium bowl and set aside for 10 minutes until it starts to bubble. Lightly whisk in the egg and milk.

In a large heatproof bowl, whisk together the semolina, flour and sugar and make a well in the centre. Pour in the egg mixture and whisk to a thick, smooth batter. Cover with plastic film and sit the bowl over a container of boiling water (it must fit snugly). Leave to prove for about 25 minutes or until the batter has doubled in size.

Melt the extra butter in a large non-stick frying pan over medium heat. Pour 2 tablespoons of batter into the pan and cook for 4 minutes (the pancake will bubble and lose its gloss when cooked through), then turn and cook the other side for 1 minute. Remove and keep warm while you cook the remaining pancakes.

To serve, top the pancakes with the banana slices, honeycomb butter and a drizzle of honey. Finish with a squeeze of lemon juice and a dusting of icing sugar, if desired.

SERVES 6–8

2 bunches asparagus, trimmed 3 cm from the bottom

100 ml extra virgin olive oil, plus extra for serving
    (optional)

sea salt and freshly ground black pepper

2 large balls buffalo mozzarella, torn into chunks

2 tablespoons plain thick yoghurt

½ red onion, finely diced

8 basil leaves, torn, plus extra to serve

2 tablespoons aged balsamic vinegar

10–12 ripe cherry tomatoes on the vine, picked

CHARGRILLED ASPARAGUS WITH CHERRY TOMATOES AND BUFFALO MOZZARELLA

The grilled asparagus gives this salad a lovely
smokiness that works perfectly with the mozzarella.
Try to buy spears that are about 1–1.5 cm thick so
they cook evenly.

Place the asparagus on a plate and drizzle with
1 tablespoon olive oil. Season with salt and pepper.

Preheat a chargrill or barbecue plate to very hot.
Grill the asparagus for 2 minutes each side, then
transfer to a serving platter.

In a small bowl, combine the mozzarella, yoghurt,
onion, basil and remaining olive oil. Season with salt
and pepper. Pour the mixture over the hot asparagus
and scatter with the extra basil leaves. Drizzle with the
balsamic vinegar and a little extra olive oil (if using)
and serve with the tomatoes.

Pictured page 242.

SERVES 8

260 g plain flour

¼ teaspoon sea salt flakes

180 g cold butter, cut into 1 cm dice

1 tablespoon iced water

2 tablespoons sour cream

Smoked trout filling

40 g butter

2 red onions, finely diced

4 cloves garlic, chopped

250 ml pouring cream

3 eggs

1 tablespoon chopped dill

sea salt and freshly ground black pepper

100 g smoked trout flakes, bones removed

30 g flaked almonds, toasted

4 big sprigs chervil

SOUR-CREAM PASTRY TART WITH SMOKED TROUT AND CARAMELISED ONION

The sour-cream pastry in this tart is fabulous – light, crumbly and deliciously savoury. Enjoy it with a chilled glass of Australian sparkling.

Sift the flour onto a clean work surface and sprinkle with the salt. Scatter the butter and water over the top and dot with the sour cream. Using the heel of your hand, work the mixture in a smooth smearing action away from you, then gather the dough and repeat until the dough comes together. There will be flecks of butter visible, but this is a good thing as it means the dough has not been overworked. Gently form the dough into a flat disc and wrap in plastic film. Rest in the fridge for 20 minutes.

Roll out the dough to fit a fluted 24 cm tart tin. Gently lift the pastry into the tin (it should be 3–4 mm thick), trim off the excess and chill for another 20 minutes. Preheat the oven to 150°C (fan-forced).

Line the pastry case with foil and fill with pastry weights or uncooked rice. Bake for 15–20 minutes until golden, then remove the foil and weights and allow to cool slightly.

To make the filling, melt the butter in a wide saucepan over medium heat and cook the onion and garlic for 10–15 minutes or until lightly caramelised. Tip into a bowl and add the cream, eggs and dill. Season with salt and pepper.

Arrange half the trout over the cooled pastry base. Pour the cream mixture evenly over the top and add the remaining trout. Sprinkle the flaked almonds over the top and press on the chervil sprigs. Bake for 15–20 minutes until golden and slightly puffed. Allow to cool slightly before serving.

Pictured page 243.

Chargrilled asparagus with cherry tomatoes and
buffalo mozzarella (see page 240)

Sour-cream pastry tart with smoked trout, caramelised onion and flaked almonds (see page 241)

3 tablespoons extra virgin olive oil

3 leeks, thinly sliced

½ brown onion, finely chopped

2 cloves garlic, finely sliced

sea salt and freshly ground black pepper

100 ml water

300 g baby spinach, washed and shredded

2½ tablespoons pouring cream

20 g butter

1 sheet puff pastry, cut into a 30 cm square

4 eggs

6 thin slices pancetta

¼ bunch chives, finely chopped

4 eggs

100 ml pouring cream

sea salt and freshly ground black pepper

1 chorizo sausage, finely chopped

2½ tablespoons olive oil

3 spring onions, finely sliced

½ handful mint leaves, chopped

½ handful flat-leaf parsley leaves, chopped

1 green chilli, sliced

4 slices sourdough bread, toasted

< GREEN EGG AND PANCETTA PUFF-PASTRY PIE

You will need a deep 24 cm springform tin and a heavy-based oven tray to make this pie.

Preheat the oven to 220°C (fan-forced).

Heat the olive oil in a saucepan over low heat. Add the leek, onion and garlic, season with salt and pepper and cook for 10 minutes. Pour in the water and cook for a further 10 minutes. Add the spinach, cream and butter and cook for 6 minutes until paste-like, then puree with a stick blender until smooth. Set aside to cool.

Place the pastry in the base of a lightly oiled 24 cm springform tin (at least 5 cm deep). Spread the leek mixture over the pastry and 3 cm up the sides. Crack the eggs on top of the leek mixture and scatter with the pancetta. Add the chives and season to taste. Roll the edges of the pastry down to the level of the pie mixture, twisting in a rope-like fashion. Place the tin on a heavy cast-iron tray that has been preheated in the oven (this will keep enough heat under the tart to cook the pastry).

Bake for 40–50 minutes or until cooked through and the pastry is golden.

SCRAMBLED EGGS WITH CHORIZO AND SPRING ONIONS

Always buy the freshest, organic free-range eggs you can find – you really will taste the difference.

Combine the eggs and cream in a bowl and season with salt and pepper.

Heat a non-stick frying pan over high heat and cook the chorizo for 3–5 minutes, stirring constantly. Reduce the heat to medium, add the olive oil and egg mixture and stir the eggs with a spatula until cooked as desired. Stir in the spring onion, mint, parsley and chilli.

Serve on hot toast.

120 g fresh ricotta, well drained

½ lemon

2 large slices sourdough bread, toasted

2 ripe figs, peeled and sliced

1 tablespoon honey

2 tablespoons unsalted pistachio kernels

2 pinches of ground cinnamon

90 g chocolate

100 g butter, softened

100 g brown sugar

1 teaspoon vanilla extract

¼ teaspoon ground nutmeg

110 g plain flour

4 eggs

100 g ground almonds

180 g raw beetroot, finely grated

50 g chocolate, melted, extra

CHOCOLATE AND BEETROOT > BROWNIES

Brownies aren't all bad. In fact, this recipe has a lot less sugar than usual and the goodness of beetroot. Just be sure to wear prep gloves when grating the beetroot or your hands will be stained bright purple!

Preheat the oven to 180°C (fan-forced). Grease and line a 10 cm × 25 cm loaf tin.

Melt the chocolate in a large heatproof bowl over a saucepan of barely simmering water (don't let the bowl touch the water). Cool to room temperature.

Cream the butter and sugar in an electric mixer, then add the vanilla, nutmeg and flour and mix well. Add the eggs one at a time, beating after each addition. Add the melted chocolate, then fold in the almonds and beetroot.

Spoon the mixture into the loaf tin and bake for 25–30 minutes or until a skewer inserted into the centre comes out clean.

Cool, then cut into small (or large!) rectangles. Melt the extra chocolate in a bowl as above and drizzle over the brownies to decorate. These are even better the day after baking.

RICOTTA ON TOAST WITH FIGS AND HONEY

This is a superb combination for a low-fat breakfast.

Place the ricotta in a bowl, add a squeeze of lemon and stir to combine.

Spread the ricotta on the toast. Top with the fig slices, drizzle with honey and sprinkle with the pistachios and cinnamon. Serve immediately.

250 g plain flour

20 g cocoa powder

2 teaspoons baking powder

160 g butter, softened

180 g raw sugar

2 large eggs

6 ripe bananas (about 500 g), mashed

60 g shredded coconut, plus 1 tablespoon
   extra, for sprinkling

100 g dark chocolate chips

1 banana, extra, sliced

CHOCOLATE AND BANANA LOAF

The combination of chocolate and banana flavours
is hard to resist. Don't toast this bread – eat it fresh.

Preheat the oven to 175°C (fan-forced). Lightly
grease a 22 cm × 12 cm loaf tin and line the base
with baking paper.

Sift the combined flour, cocoa and baking powder
into a bowl.

Beat the butter and sugar in an electric mixer until
light and fluffy. Add the eggs one at a time, beating
well between additions. Add the mashed banana and
stir until combined. Fold in the flour mixture, then
add the coconut and chocolate chips and stir until
well combined.

Spoon the mixture into the tin and arrange the extra
banana slices and coconut over the top. Bake for
1 hour or until a skewer inserted into the centre comes
out clean. Cool in the tin for 15 minutes then turn out
onto a wire rack to cool completely.

SERVES 6–8

250 g dried great northern beans

120 ml olive oil

1 brown onion, diced

1 leek, sliced

5 cloves garlic, finely chopped

5 sprigs thyme

1 tablespoon brown mustard seeds

3 tablespoons cider vinegar

3 tablespoons brown sugar

2 tablespoons curry powder

1 × 400 g can crushed tomatoes

600 ml tomato passata

1 tablespoon tomato paste (puree)

1 vegetable stock cube

600 ml boiling water

sea salt

toasted sourdough bread, to serve

1 ripe avocado, stone removed and thickly sliced

120 g feta, crumbled

extra virgin olive oil, for drizzling (optional)

tarragon sprigs, to serve (optional)

BAKED BEANS WITH MUSTARD SEEDS, VINEGAR AND TOMATO

I love homemade baked beans on toast, and the sugar and spice in this version give it an interesting twist. A generous serve will definitely keep you focused until lunch time.

Soak the beans in hot water overnight. Drain, then place the beans in a large saucepan, cover with water and boil for 30 minutes. Drain.

Heat the olive oil in a large heavy-based saucepan and cook the onion, leek, garlic and thyme for 3 minutes. Add the beans, mustard seeds, vinegar, sugar, curry powder, crushed tomatoes, passata and tomato paste. Dissolve the stock cube in the boiling water, add to the pan and bring to the simmer. Cook for 40 minutes until the beans are tender, then season generously with salt.

Pile the baked beans on toast and serve with avocado slices and crumbled feta. Finish with a drizzle of olive oil, if liked, and sprinkle with fresh tarragon, if available.

TOTALLY PREPPED
SUNDAY LUNCH

FRIED EGG IN BRIK PASTRY WITH CAPER
AND PARSLEY SALAD AND HOT CHILLI SAUCE

SNAPPER, SCALLOP, CLAM AND POTATO BAKE

SLOW-BAKED APPLE PIE

SERVES 4

6 desiree or dutch cream potatoes

½ head curly endive, washed

400 g small clams

100 ml white wine

4 tablespoons olive oil

500 g white fish fillets, skin and bones removed,
    cut into 3 cm pieces

300 g cleaned scallops

½ cup (80 g) fresh peas

40 g butter

80 g grated parmesan

White sauce

60 g butter

2 cloves garlic, finely sliced

60 g plain flour

600 ml hot fish stock

100 ml pouring cream

sea salt and freshly ground black pepper

SNAPPER, SCALLOP, CLAM AND POTATO BAKE

This recipe is based on English-style fish pies made with white sauce. The addition of clams and a veloute-style sauce with peas and endive give an old favourite a new lease on life.

To make the white sauce, melt the butter in a medium saucepan and cook the garlic for 2 minutes. Stir in the flour until it starts to bubble, then swap to a whisk. Gradually pour in the hot fish stock, whisking constantly, and cook for 2 minutes until thickened. Stir in the cream, salt and lots of black pepper, then set aside to cool.

Boil the potatoes for 15 minutes or until tender. Drain and cut into 1 cm thick rounds.

Blanch the endive in salted boiling water for about 3 minutes, then drain and roughly chop.

Preheat the oven to 200°C (fan-forced).

Place the clams and white wine in a saucepan and steam for 3 minutes until the shells have opened. Remove most of the clams from the shells, reserving about half the juices (leave a few in their shells for presentation purposes).

Heat the olive oil in a large frying pan over high heat, add the fish and quickly brown on all sides (this should only take a minute at the most). Drain on paper towel. Repeat with the scallops.

Add the clams, fish pieces, scallops, peas, endive and the reserved clam juices to the white sauce and mix well. Transfer to a medium round or oval baking dish that is 5–7 cm deep. Layer the potato slices over the clam mixture, overlapping slightly, and top with the butter and parmesan. Bake for 30 minutes or until golden.

SERVES 1

1 round brik pastry

1 large egg

sea salt and freshly ground black pepper

1 tablespoon capers

4 tablespoons olive oil

1 handful flat-leaf parsley leaves, torn

¼ bulb fennel, shaved

¼ red onion, finely chopped (optional)

1 tablespoon hot chilli sauce

FRIED EGG IN BRIK PASTRY WITH CAPER AND PARSLEY SALAD AND HOT CHILLI SAUCE

I used to eat this wonderful concoction at my grandmother's house. Brik pastry is a thin Tunisian pastry that comes in rounds similar to wonton wrappers. It is available from specialist food stores and Middle Eastern delicatessens.

Place the pastry on a dinner plate. Crack the egg into the centre of the pastry and season with salt and pepper. Add half the capers, then carefully fold the pastry edges inwards to form a square pocket.

Heat the olive oil in a non-stick frying pan over medium heat. Add the pastry, seam-side down, and cook for 2–3 minutes. Turn over and cook until the pastry is golden and the egg is cooked to your liking.

To serve, scatter the parsley, fennel, onion (if using) and remaining capers over the pastry. Drizzle with chilli sauce.

Pictured page 252.

SERVES 4–6

25 g butter, softened

900 g red apples, peeled, cored and sliced
    (I love cox's orange pippin)

145 g raw sugar, plus 30 g extra for sprinkling (optional)

5 cloves

1½ tablespoons cornflour

juice of 1 lemon

450 g puff pastry

1 tablespoon thickened cream, plus extra to serve

SLOW-BAKED APPLE PIE >

You must try this traditional pie. It scents the whole house as it cooks.

Preheat the oven to 180°C (fan-forced). Use the butter to grease a round 20 cm × 5 cm springform tin. Line a baking tray with baking paper and place the tin on top.

Mix the apple, sugar, cloves, cornflour and lemon juice in a large bowl.

Roll out two-thirds of the puff pastry until it is just under 1 cm thick. Line the tin with the pastry, allowing a little pastry to hang over the edge. Fill with the apple mixture and gently press to flatten.

Roll out the remaining pastry to form a 22 cm round. Brush the edge with cream, then invert the round and place on top of the apple. Press the pastry edge together, then trim the excess and press with a fork to seal. Brush the pastry top with the remaining cream, sprinkle with the extra sugar if liked and use a knife to cut a few holes in the lid for the steam to escape.

Bake the pie for 30 minutes. Reduce the temperature to 150°C (fan-forced) and bake for a further 40 minutes or until the crust is golden and the apple mixture is bubbling. Cool slightly in the tin on a wire rack. Serve warm with a dollop of cream.

HOT SUMMER NIGHT

SPINACH, ZUCCHINI AND PEA FRITTERS WITH
PRAWNS AND PRESERVED LEMON DRESSING

KOUSHARY

SNAPPER SPICED WITH BAHARAT AND GARLIC

FRESH TOMATO AND LIME CHUTNEY

WATERMELON AND RASPBERRY SALAD
WITH ROSEWATER AND YOGHURT SORBET

SERVES 6–8 AS A STARTER

1 teaspoon chopped garlic

2 tablespoons extra virgin olive oil

2 teaspoons ground cumin

2 tablespoons ground coriander

½ teaspoon chilli powder

170 g chickpea flour

280 ml cold water

¾ teaspoon baking powder

80 g cornflour

300 g baby spinach, shredded

2 zucchini (courgettes), grated and squeezed
   to remove excess juice

3 spring onions, finely sliced diagonally

1 small red onion, finely chopped

½ cup (60 g) frozen peas, thawed

120 ml vegetable oil

24 cooked peeled prawns

nigella seeds, to serve (optional)

lemon wedges, to serve (optional)

Preserved lemon dressing

½ cup (140 g) plain yoghurt

1 teaspoon finely chopped preserved lemon rind

½ teaspoon ground cumin

juice of ½ lemon

SPINACH, ZUCCHINI AND PEA FRITTERS WITH PRAWNS AND PRESERVED LEMON DRESSING

Everyone loves a fritter and these are particularly good. Serve them straight from the pan, with a sprinkle of salt and a squeeze of lemon. Chickpea flour is available from selected supermarkets, health-food stores and Indian grocery stores. Nigella seeds can be found in food halls and speciality spice shops.

Combine the garlic, olive oil, cumin, coriander, chilli powder, chickpea flour, water, baking powder and cornflour in a very large mixing bowl and whisk to a smooth batter. In a separate bowl, combine the spinach, zucchini, spring onion, red onion and peas. Add the spinach mixture to the batter and stir well.

For the dressing, place all the ingredients in a bowl and stir to combine.

Heat the vegetable oil in a large non-stick frying pan over high heat. When hot, add 2 tablespoons of batter per fritter and cook for 2–3 minutes each side or until golden. Remove and drain on paper towel. Keep warm while you make the remaining fritters.

To serve, arrange the fritters on a platter and top with the prawns and yoghurt dressing. Sprinkle with nigella seeds and serve with lemon wedges, if desired.

Pictured page 258.

SERVES 6–8

2½ tablespoons vegetable oil

120 g rice vermicelli, broken

500 g basmati rice

2 pinches of sea salt

900 ml boiling water

100 g butter

1 tablespoon nigella seeds

KOUSHARY

This delicious side dish also goes well with fish or
vegetable curries of Egyptian origin.

Heat the oil in a medium heavy-based saucepan
over medium heat. Add the vermicelli and cook for
3–5 minutes until lightly browned and coated with the
oil. Add the rice and salt and stir to coat with the oil.

Add the boiling water and cook, covered, for about
15–20 minutes, stirring occasionally with a fork and
adding more water if necessary. Stir through the butter
and allow to rest for 5 minutes. Sprinkle with nigella
seeds just before serving.

Pictured page 263.

SERVES 6

1.8–2 kg snapper, gutted, cleaned and scaled
   (ask your fishmonger to do this)
100 ml extra virgin olive oil
6 cloves garlic, thinly sliced
sea salt and freshly ground black pepper
1 tablespoon baharat
2 lemons
fennel fronds, to serve (optional)

SERVES 4–6 AS AN ACCOMPANIMENT

10 large tomatoes, diced
juice of 2 limes
½ teaspoon dried chilli flakes
2 teaspoons brown sugar
2 teaspoons sea salt
1 teaspoon celery seeds
½ large red onion, finely chopped
6 cm piece ginger, finely sliced

SNAPPER SPICED WITH BAHARAT AND GARLIC

Fish cooked on the bone is in a class of its own. It is tender and retains its pure flavour.

Preheat the oven to 220°C (fan-forced).

Dry the fish inside and out with clean paper towel and score two or three times on each side. Rub both sides with some of the olive oil and insert the garlic in the cuts. Season and rub with the baharat.

Tear off three 60 cm lengths of foil and lay over a 60 cm piece of baking paper. Place the fish on top then squeeze over the juice of two lemons and drizzle with the remaining olive oil. Lift the foil and paper sides up over the fish and seal by folding it over several times. Transfer to a large baking tray and bake for 40–50 minutes (or cook in a lidded barbecue). Remove and rest for 5 minutes before serving.

FRESH TOMATO AND LIME CHUTNEY

I really like this sharp limey chutney, particularly with the pristine flavour of fish cooked on the bone. It also goes well with any Indian curry.

Combine all the ingredients in a bowl. Stir to combine, then set aside to rest for 10 minutes.

SERVES 6

120 g caster sugar

3 tablespoons water

2 teaspoons rosewater

10 lychees, peeled and seeded

½ watermelon

300 g fresh raspberries

6 scoops yoghurt sorbet (or use vanilla ice-cream)

2 handfuls unsprayed delicate pink rose petals

WATERMELON AND RASPBERRY SALAD WITH ROSEWATER AND YOGHURT SORBET

Take a refreshing look at fruit through rose-coloured glasses with this exotic fruit salad. You can easily double or triple the recipe and it will still present beautifully. If fresh raspberries are a bit pricey use strawberries or blackberries or whatever berries are at their seasonal best.

Place the sugar and water in a small saucepan that is scrupulously clean and bring to a quick boil for 1 minute or until the sugar has dissolved. Set aside to cool for 5 minutes. Remove from the heat and stir in the rosewater and lychees, then leave to steep for 5 minutes.

Using a large melon baller, make as many balls as you can from the watermelon. Pile them up into a stack on a chilled platter and scatter the raspberries over the top. Arrange the scoops of sorbet over the fruit then spoon over the rosewater and lychee syrup. Scatter with the petals and serve as soon as possible in chilled bowls.

CHRISTMAS DINNER

HAM HOCK TERRINE WITH
PARSLEY AND LENTILS

TROFIE WITH PRAWNS, LEEK,
LEMON AND BOTTARGA

ROAST PARSNIP WITH WHITE SWEET POTATO

ROAST DUCK WITH RHUBARB
AND GINGER RELISH

COLD CITRUS SOUFFLE WITH
RASPBERRY TOFFEE SAUCE

CHERRY, RASPBERRY AND VANILLA JAM

2 meaty ham hocks (about 900 g each)

1 large bulb garlic, halved

2 carrots

1 brown onion, halved

2 sticks celery

1 tablespoon black peppercorns

1 bunch flat-leaf parsley, leaves and stems finely chopped

1 bay leaf

5 sprigs thyme

100 g Australian puy lentils

600 ml chicken stock

3 leaves gold-strength gelatine

1 tablespoon extra virgin olive oil

2 leeks, trimmed and finely diced

4 cloves garlic, extra, sliced

8 small cornichons, finely chopped

2 tablespoons baby capers, drained

sea salt and freshly ground black pepper

3 teaspoons sherry vinegar

ciabatta and pickles, to serve

Horseradish cream

3 tablespoons grated fresh horseradish
   (or half this if using horseradish from a jar)

200 ml creme fraiche or sour cream

pinch of salt

HAM HOCK TERRINE WITH PARSLEY AND LENTILS

This is my take on a classic French terrine. Make it the day before as it needs to be chilled overnight.

Place the ham hocks in a large saucepan with enough water to cover. Add the garlic, carrots, onion, celery, peppercorns, parsley stems, bay leaf and thyme and simmer over medium heat for 2 hours (add more water if required as the hock needs to be submerged in liquid the whole time). When the meat is tender and springs back from the bones, transfer the hocks to a bowl and cool slightly.

Meanwhile, place the lentils and chicken stock in a small saucepan and simmer for 15–20 minutes until tender. Drain.

Soak the gelatine leaves in cold water until soft, then squeeze to remove any excess water.

When the ham hocks are cool enough to handle, pull the meat from the bones and cut into large chunks, including a little of the soft, sticky tendons. Strain the cooking liquid into a clean saucepan, discarding the solids, and bring to the boil. Cook until reduced by two-thirds then strain again and set aside. Add the gelatine leaves, stir and strain into a jug (you should have 350–500 ml liquid).

Heat the olive oil in a frying pan and cook the leek and garlic over low heat for 5–8 minutes or until softened but not coloured. Set aside.

Line a 30 cm × 6 cm terrine mould with plastic film, sprinkle in a third of the chopped parsley leaves and refrigerate.

In a medium bowl, combine the ham chunks, lentils, cornichons, capers, remaining parsley and leek and garlic mixture. Season with salt and pepper and the vinegar – the terrine should be highly seasoned as the intensity dies back when set and chilled.

Spoon half the ham mixture into the terrine mould and pour over half the liquid. Spoon in the remaining mixture and pour over a little more of the liquid to just cover. Chill overnight to set.

To make the horseradish cream, place all the ingredients in a bowl and mix together well.

Remove the terrine from the mould and serve with fresh ciabatta, horseradish cream and pickles.

500 g trofie pasta

100 ml extra virgin olive oil

16 raw prawns, peeled, butterflied and cut
    into small pieces (reserve half the heads)

sea salt and freshly ground black pepper

2 leeks, trimmed and sliced into rings

5 cloves garlic, thinly sliced

1½ teaspoons fennel seeds, lightly crushed

100 g butter

juice of 1 lemon

60 g bottarga, shaved

3 parsnips, peeled and each cut lengthways
    into 6 pieces (remove cores if woody)

2 white sweet potatoes, peeled, cut into 2 cm rounds

1 cinnamon stick

½ teaspoon grated nutmeg

1 small bulb garlic, bruised

5 sprigs thyme

sea salt and freshly ground black pepper

100 ml extra virgin olive oil

100 ml water

< TROFIE WITH PRAWNS, LEEK, LEMON AND BOTTARGA

A perfect balance of flavours, this pasta dish combines the lovely sweetness of the leeks with the richness of the bottarga (cured fish roe). If trofie is unavailable, any other tiny spiral pasta will work just as well.

Cook the pasta in plenty of lightly salted boiling water until al dente.

Meanwhile, heat the olive oil in a large heavy-based saucepan, add the prawn heads and cook until they change colour. Season with salt and pepper, then squeeze all the tasty juices into the pan. Discard the heads.

Add the leek, garlic and fennel seeds and cook over low heat for 10 minutes until the leek has softened. Stir in the chopped prawns and cook for 2 minutes.

Drain the pasta well and add to the prawn mixture. Stir in the butter and lemon juice and season to taste. Top with the shaved bottarga and serve.

ROAST PARSNIP WITH WHITE SWEET POTATO

White-fleshed sweet potato has bright purple skin and when roasted has a delicious nutty flavour similar to cooked chestnuts. Great as a side dish instead of fries or regular roast potatoes.

Preheat the oven to 200°C (fan-forced).

Place all the ingredients (except the water) in a large bowl and toss to combine.

Transfer to a baking tray and sprinkle with the water. Cover with foil and roast for 20 minutes. Remove the foil and roast for a further 5 minutes or until golden and cooked through.

Pictured page 266.

2.5 kg duck, excess skin and fat trimmed

sea salt and freshly ground black pepper

2 large brown onions, skin on, cut into rounds

fresh red currants, to serve (optional)

Rhubarb and ginger relish

10 sticks rhubarb, trimmed and sliced
  on the diagonal

8 cm piece ginger, cut into matchsticks

180 g brown sugar

1 tablespoon black peppercorns, crushed

3 tablespoons sherry or red wine vinegar

10 sprigs thyme, leaves picked

2 teaspoons sea salt

ROAST DUCK WITH RHUBARB AND GINGER RELISH

This is a really luscious dish – roasting the duck twice makes the meat tender and the skin crispy.

Preheat the oven to 200°C (fan-forced).

Season the duck with salt and pepper inside and out and bring to room temperature. Place the onion rounds in a baking dish, sit the duck on top and roast for 1 hour. Remove and set aside for 30 minutes.

Meanwhile, to make the relish, place all the ingredients in a 24 cm × 34 cm baking dish in a single layer. Mix to combine and set aside for 15 minutes.

Put the relish in the oven at the same time as the duck and bake for 10 minutes. Remove from the oven and gently stir, then bake for a further 15 minutes or until the rhubarb is tender. Remove from the oven and leave to cool without stirring. (Once cooled, place it in the fridge if not using immediately, then bring it back to room temperature before serving.)

Line a baking tray with baking paper and place the roast duck on a board. Run a knife down each side of the breastbone along the length of the breast. Using your fingers and the knife, cut or push the meat away from the ribcage, working down and around. Separate the wing bone from the ribcage and work down towards the leg, pushing it out slightly. Separate the thigh bone from the body. Repeat on the other side, keeping all the meat and skin attached. Discard the carcass. Transfer the duck halves to the baking tray then place, uncovered, in the fridge.

Close to serving time, preheat the oven to 200°C (fan-forced). Season the duck well with salt and roast on the tray, skin-side up, for 20 minutes. Remove from the oven and cut each half into four pieces. Serve with the rhubarb relish, garnished with red currants (if you're lucky enough to find them).

5 large eggs, separated

180 g caster sugar

finely grated zest and juice of 4 lemons

3½ leaves titanium-strength gelatine

2½ tablespoons hot water

500 ml pouring cream, lightly whipped

2 tablespoons crystallised ginger, chopped

200 g fresh raspberries

Raspberry toffee sauce

200 g caster sugar

2½ tablespoons water

300 g frozen raspberries

juice of ½ lemon

COLD CITRUS SOUFFLE WITH RASPBERRY TOFFEE SAUCE

Place the egg yolks, sugar, lemon zest and lemon juice in a large bowl over a saucepan of simmering water and whisk until thick and pale. Remove from the heat.

Soak the gelatine leaves in cold water until soft, then squeeze to remove any excess water. Place the leaves in a bowl with the hot water and stir to dissolve. Add the gelatine liquid to the yolk mixture and whisk until smooth. Place in the fridge for 20–25 minutes until cold and starting to set. Stir in the cream, then chill again until slightly set.

Whisk the egg whites until stiff peaks form, then fold into the yolk mixture with the ginger. Spoon the mixture into six or eight glasses and chill for 2 hours.

To make the sauce, combine the sugar and water in a small saucepan over low heat and stir until the sugar has dissolved. Increase the heat and boil until the mixture is a caramel colour. Pour immediately into a food processor with the frozen raspberries and lemon juice and process to a smooth sauce. Pour into a jug and refrigerate until the sauce is chilled.

Pour the sauce over the souffles and top with raspberries.

1.8 kg cherries, pitted (to produce about 1.5 kg), stones reserved

1.4 kg caster sugar

2 vanilla beans, seeds scraped and bean chopped

thinly peeled zest and juice of 1 lemon

12 apricot kernels, chopped (optional)

600 g frozen raspberries

juice of 1 lemon

CHERRY, RASPBERRY AND VANILLA JAM

This jam is ideal to give away as a festive gift. To ensure a perfect finished product, it is worth making a batch of this jam no smaller than the recipe specifies.

Tie the reserved cherry stones in a clean square of muslin and place in a large heavy-based saucepan with the cherries, sugar, vanilla bean, lemon zest and apricot kernels (if using). Stir over very low heat until the cherries have released their juices and the sugar has dissolved.

Bring to the boil and cook for 45 minutes. Add the raspberries and lemon juice and cook for a further 10–15 minutes or until cooked. (To check, place a small amount on a chilled saucer – it should set.)

Remove the cherry stones and lemon zest. Spoon the jam into hot sterilised jars (see page 114) and seal when cool.

CHRISTMAS BUFFET EXTRAVAGANZA

PRAWN AND PARSLEY MAYONNAISE
ON TOASTED BAGUETTE

OCEAN TROUT FILLET WITH MINT LABNA

SPICED CHICKEN, QUAIL
AND PISTACHIO TERRINE

ORZO WITH CRAYFISH, PEAS AND SORREL

SABA-GLAZED HAM WITH PICKLED CHERRIES

NOUGAT CASSATA

SHERRY AND CHERRY TRIFLE

CHOUX RING WITH RAISIN
CREAM AND TOFFEE SAUCE

SERVES 12 (EASILY DOUBLED)

1 baguette, cut into 1 cm thick slices
½ lemon, very finely sliced (optional)
watercress and caviar, to garnish (optional)

Prawn and parsley mayonnaise
14 large cooked king prawns, peeled,
    deveined and chopped
3 hard-boiled eggs, chopped
¼ bunch flat-leaf parsley, leaves picked
    and very finely chopped
4 spring onions, very finely sliced
splash of Tabasco sauce
pinch of sea salt
3 tablespoons whole-egg mayonnaise
2 tablespoons plain yoghurt
½ teaspoon sugar

PRAWN AND PARSLEY MAYONNAISE ON TOASTED BAGUETTE

I've used prawns here, but this mayonnaise mix would work just as well with crab, crayfish or a seafood medley.

Toast the baguette slices on both sides under a grill or in a low oven until crisp. Set aside.

To make the prawn and parsley mayonnaise, combine all the ingredients in a bowl and stir well. Cover with plastic film and chill until ready to serve.

Spread the prawn mixture on the toasts and top with the lemon slices (if using). Garnish with watercress and caviar if desired and serve immediately.

SERVES 4

1½ cups (420 g) plain Greek-style yoghurt
1.2 kg ocean trout fillet, skin on, all bones removed
sea salt and freshly ground black pepper
2½ tablespoons extra virgin olive oil
½ bunch mint, leaves picked and coarsely chopped
1 clove garlic, finely chopped or grated
2 teaspoons coriander seeds, toasted and lightly crushed
juice of 1 small lemon
4 spring onions, finely sliced
150 g walnuts, toasted and coarsely chopped
1 bunch sorrel, finely shredded, to garnish (optional)
3 tablespoons pomegranate molasses
lemon wedges, to serve

OCEAN TROUT FILLET WITH MINT LABNA

Ask your fishmonger for the head end of the ocean trout. If you are serving this on its own, it's lovely with steamed couscous and a simple green salad.

Preheat the oven to 220°C (fan-forced). Line a baking tray with a sheet of baking paper. Place the yoghurt in a muslin-lined sieve over a bowl and drain for 30 minutes.

Place the fish on the baking tray, season with salt and pepper and drizzle with olive oil. Wrap in the baking paper, folding in the edges to seal the trout tightly. Bake for 12 minutes or until cooked through (18 minutes if you like it well done), then leave to rest, wrapped, for at least 8 minutes. It should be cooked pink rare.

In a bowl, combine the drained yoghurt with the mint, garlic, coriander seeds, lemon juice and a little salt.

Place the fish on a serving platter. Spread the labna over the top, then sprinkle with the spring onion and walnuts, pressing the nuts gently onto the fish. Arrange the sorrel around the platter (if using) and drizzle with the pomegranate molasses. Serve with lemon wedges.

Pictured page 280.

Ocean trout fillet with mint labna (see page 279)

Spiced chicken, quail and pistachio terrine
(see page 283)

150 g chicken livers, trimmed and chopped

150 ml milk

200 g fatty Serrano prosciutto, thinly sliced

½ bunch flat-leaf parsley, leaves picked

½ bunch coriander, leaves picked

100 g unsalted butter

6 cloves garlic, finely chopped

3 large golden shallots, finely chopped

2 teaspoons ground cumin

2 teaspoons ground coriander

2 teaspoons ground allspice

3 tablespoons cognac

1 tablespoon extra virgin olive oil

sea salt and freshly ground black pepper

4 quails (about 350 g), fully boned

2 × 250 g chicken thigh fillets, skin on,
cut into 2 cm pieces

2 × 350 g chicken breast fillets, skin removed,
cut into 3 cm pieces

6 sprigs thyme, leaves picked

1 tablespoon sea salt

1 teaspoon freshly ground black pepper

1½ teaspoons finely chopped preserved lemon rind

1 cup (175 g) pistachios, shelled

200 g pork mince

1 large egg, beaten

1 tablespoon green peppercorns

¾ cup (50 g) fresh breadcrumbs, made from day-old bread

Sultana chutney

2 tablespoons extra virgin olive oil

6 cloves garlic, thinly sliced

2 teaspoons fennel seeds, toasted and
coarsely ground

1 celery heart, finely sliced

sea salt and freshly ground black pepper

2½ tablespoons sherry vinegar

2½ tablespoons water

120 g sugar

1 tablespoon sea salt flakes

150 g Iranian golden sultanas

5 golden shallots, sliced

2 small red chillies, finely sliced

1 green chilli, seeds removed and sliced

1 tablespoon finely chopped preserved lemon rind

4 large lemons, segmented and chopped into small
triangles (retain the juice)

SPICED CHICKEN, QUAIL AND PISTACHIO TERRINE

Make this light but full-flavoured terrine at least a day or two in advance. Well wrapped, it will keep in the fridge for about a week – just bring it to room temperature before serving.

Soak the chicken livers in the milk for 15 minutes, then drain and dry on paper towel. Set aside.

Preheat the oven to 170°C (fan-forced). Line a 10 cm × 30 cm terrine with the prosciutto, with pieces overlapping and hanging over the edges.

Place the parsley and coriander in a saucepan of salted boiling water for 15 seconds, then drain and refresh in cold water. Squeeze out the excess liquid and chop roughly. Set aside.

Melt half the butter in a large frying pan over medium heat. Add the garlic and shallots and cook for about 3 minutes. Increase the heat, add the spices and livers and cook for 1 minute. Stir in the cognac, then remove the pan from the heat and tip the mixture into a large bowl. Set aside.

Wipe out the pan with paper towel, then add the olive oil and remaining butter. Season the quails, then brown, skin-side down, for 2 minutes. Remove and dice. Season the chicken thigh and breast meat, then saute over high heat for 2–3 minutes. Add the quail and chicken to the liver mixture with the remaining ingredients and mix thoroughly with your hands.

Place the mixture in the terrine, pressing down well, then fold over the prosciutto to enclose. Cover with baking paper and foil, and place in a baking dish. Pour boiling water into the dish to come halfway up the terrine. Bake for 55 minutes or until the juices run clear when tested with a skewer. Remove the terrine from the baking dish, cool slightly then weigh down with foil-wrapped cardboard and three 400 g cans and refrigerate overnight. Bring to room temperature about half an hour before serving.

To make the chutney, place the olive oil and garlic in a small saucepan over medium heat and cook gently until the garlic starts to colour. Add the fennel seeds and the celery and season. Reduce the heat to low and cook, stirring, for 1 minute then remove from the heat.

Combine the vinegar, water, sugar and salt in a small saucepan over medium heat and bring to the boil. Add the sultanas, shallots and red and green chilli and cook for 6 minutes. Stir in the preserved lemon and fresh lemon and simmer gently for 2 minutes. Add the garlic and fennel mixture and cook for another minute. Serve with the terrine or pour the chutney into a sterilised jar (see page 114) and save it for another time.

Pictured page 281.

SERVES 4–6

2 small cooked crayfish (about 1.2 kg each)

200 ml extra virgin olive oil, plus extra to serve

2 cloves garlic, smashed

4 golden shallots, peeled and sliced

2 teaspoons fennel seeds

4 good-quality anchovies

sea salt

1 bunch flat-leaf parsley, stems and leaves
coarsely chopped

4 ripe tomatoes, diced with skin and seeds

1 teaspoon tomato paste (puree)

1 lemon, sliced

300 ml white wine

1 litre fish or chicken stock

500 ml water

2 tablespoons raw sugar

500 g orzo pasta

200 g fresh peas

2 teaspoons caster sugar

3 cloves garlic, extra, sliced

1½ tablespoons dried chilli flakes

50 g cold unsalted butter, diced

juice of 1 lemon

6 sorrel leaves, cut into thin strips (optional)

ORZO WITH CRAYFISH, PEAS AND SORREL

The fresh peas give a burst of sweetness and a bright colour to this dish. The sorrel's lemon flavour is a perfect match with the crayfish.

Remove the crayfish heads, chop them into large pieces and set aside for later. Chop each tail into four medallion sections with the shell on and remove the entrails as you go. Remove the meat from the legs and leave whole, if possible.

Heat 2½ tablespoons olive oil in a large heavy-based saucepan over high heat and cook the crayfish head pieces for 3 minutes, stirring constantly. Add the smashed garlic cloves, shallot, fennel seeds, anchovies and a pinch of salt, and cook for 1 minute. Add the parsley, tomatoes, tomato paste and lemon and cook for 1 minute. Pour in the wine and boil for 3 minutes, then add the stock and water and bring to a simmer. Add the sugar and another pinch of salt.

Simmer for 25 minutes, then strain the liquid into a clean saucepan and discard the solids. Cook the stock over medium heat for 15 minutes or until reduced by half. Strain through a fine strainer and set aside.

Cook the pasta in plenty of lightly salted boiling water until al dente. Drain.

In a large mortar and pestle, pound half the peas (starting with a few at a time) with sugar and a little salt. Add 100 ml olive oil and pound to a rough paste. Alternatively, pulse in a food processor.

Heat the remaining olive oil in a large, heavy-based saucepan over medium heat. Add the sliced garlic, chilli and crayfish meat. Stir, season with salt and cook for 2 minutes. Pour in 800 ml of the reduced stock and bring to a simmer, then remove from the heat.

Add the pasta to the pan. Add the pea mix, reserved peas, butter and a little extra olive oil and stir briefly until warmed through. Transfer to a serving platter, and finish with lemon juice and a scattering of sorrel strips (if using). Serve immediately.

6 kg organic ham on the bone

2 branches bay leaves, plus 1 branch extra

½ bunch thyme

½ bunch flat-leaf parsley, plus 4 sprigs extra

4 sprigs rosemary, plus 2 sprigs extra

4 tablespoons peppercorns

3 bulbs garlic, halved

3 tablespoons fennel seeds

4 sticks celery

grated zest of 2 oranges

10 kipfler or dutch cream potatoes, peeled

olive oil, for coating

sea salt and freshly ground black pepper

3 tablespoons cloves

2–3 onions, cut in half

Saba glaze

200 ml saba

50 ml verjuice

Pickled cherries

4 tablespoons sea salt

100 ml verjuice

2 red shallots, sliced

15 grinds black pepper

150 g raw sugar

1 bay leaf

1 clove garlic, sliced

100 ml red wine vinegar

180 g cherry jam

400 g cherries, pitted

SABA-GLAZED HAM WITH PICKLED CHERRIES

This delicate ham will keep in the fridge for at least 10 days. If you don't have a pan big enough to fit a whole ham, you can buy large upright boiling pots at chefs' warehouses and restaurant and catering suppliers.

Place the ham, bay leaves, thyme, parsley, rosemary, peppercorns, garlic, fennel seeds, celery, orange zest and enough cold water to cover in a very large saucepan. Bring to a simmer and cook for 1½ hours, rotating the ham every 30 minutes to submerge.

Preheat the oven to 200°C (fan-forced).

Place the potatoes in a saucepan of water and bring to the boil. Drain and toss in olive oil, season with salt and pepper and roast for 50 minutes until crisp and golden, stirring occasionally.

Meanwhile, remove the ham from the pan and place in a very large baking dish with the onion halves and extra herbs. Cut around the cuff of the ham and peel away the skin, leaving the fat on. Score the fat in a pinstripe pattern and stud with the cloves.

For the glaze, mix together the saba and verjuice.

Baste the ham with half the glaze and roast for 30 minutes, then baste with the remaining glaze. Increase the oven temperature to 250°C (fan-forced), or turn on the grill, and cook the ham for 5–10 minutes until caramelised on top.

For the pickled cherries, combine all the ingredients, except the cherries, in a medium saucepan over high heat. Stir well and bring to a simmer. Add the cherries, stir and cook for 5 minutes. Allow to cool.

Serve the ham with the pickled cherries, roast potatoes and any extra saba glaze, if desired.

SERVES 8–10

500 ml best-quality chocolate ice-cream, softened

2 tablespoons honey

110 g sugar

1 tablespoon water

3 large egg whites

60 g firm rose Turkish delight, cut into 5 mm pieces

50 g unsalted pistachios, shelled

50 g blanched almonds, toasted

2 tablespoons rosewater

½ teaspoon vanilla extract

50 g glace cherries

30 g crystallised angelica, finely chopped (optional)

500 ml good-quality vanilla ice-cream, softened

100 ml thickened cream

4 tablespoons marsala

4 tablespoons amaretto liqueur

20 savoiardi biscuits

unsprayed pink rose petals, to decorate (optional)

NOUGAT CASSATA

The cassata will keep for 4–5 days in the freezer – decorate it just before serving. For a further festive touch, toss pitted cherries in rosewater and a splash of amaretto, then dust them with icing sugar and serve as an accompaniment.

Line a 26 cm fluted loose-based flan tin with 5 cm deep sides with two layers of plastic film, leaving some overhanging. Tip the chocolate ice-cream into the flan tin, smooth the surface and place in the freezer overnight.

Combine the honey, sugar and water in a small, clean stainless-steel saucepan over medium heat and stir until the sugar has dissolved. Increase the heat and boil for 5 minutes until the mixture reaches 115°C on a sugar thermometer (or medium–small bubbles appear).

Meanwhile, put the egg whites in a clean electric mixer and whisk until soft peaks form. With the motor running at high speed, slowly pour in the hot sugar syrup and whisk for 5 minutes or until the bowl feels cool. Stir in the Turkish delight, pistachios, almonds, rosewater, vanilla, glace cherries and angelica (if using).

Tip the vanilla ice-cream into a large bowl and add the cream. Gently fold in the nougat mixture, then pour evenly over the chocolate ice-cream in the tin.

Place the marsala and amaretto in a shallow bowl. Quickly dip the biscuits in the liquid, then arrange on top of the nougat, filling all gaps. (You may need to crush some biscuits and sprinkle into the gaps.) Cover with plastic film and freeze for at least 6 hours.

To serve, unmould the cassata onto a plate. If you have unsprayed rose petals, use to garnish. Serve immediately.

SERVES 8

950 g cherries, pitted (to produce about 800 g),
   plus extra to garnish
150 g caster sugar
200 ml dry sherry, plus extra for dipping biscuits
2 tablespoons cherry jam
9 leaves titanium-strength gelatine
140 g cherry jam, extra
3 tablespoons water
10–12 savoiardi biscuits, halved lengthways
50 g marzipan, chopped into 5 mm pieces
250 ml pouring cream, whipped
toasted flaked almonds, to serve (optional)
icing sugar, to serve (optional)

Custard
1 vanilla bean, split and seeds scraped
150 g caster sugar
finely grated zest of ½ lemon
4 tablespoons cornflour
6 egg yolks
675 ml milk
450 ml pouring cream

SHERRY AND CHERRY TRIFLE

If you're super-organised, you can make this trifle the day before – the flavours will improve overnight.

Place the cherries, sugar and sherry in a large saucepan over medium heat. Bring to a simmer, then reduce the heat to low and cook for 2–3 minutes. Remove three-quarters of the cherries and set aside. Add the cherry jam to the pan and simmer for 2 minutes, then strain to produce about 600 ml of liquid (if you don't have enough, add a little water and boil again briefly). Return the liquid to the pan.

Meanwhile, soak the gelatine leaves in cold water until soft, then squeeze to remove any excess water. Add the gelatine to the cherry mixture and stir to dissolve. Strain half the liquid into a large glass serving dish.

Pour the rest into a small dish to a depth of about 1 cm. Cover both dishes and chill in the fridge until set.

For the custard, combine the vanilla seeds, sugar, lemon zest and cornflour in a large bowl. Whisk in the egg yolks. Combine the milk, cream and vanilla bean in a medium saucepan and simmer over low heat for about 2 minutes. Remove the bean, then add the milk mixture to the egg mixture and stir until smooth. Transfer to a saucepan and stir over low heat until the custard thickens to coat the back of a wooden spoon. Pour into a bowl and chill.

Combine the extra cherry jam and water in a small saucepan and simmer for 1 minute. Set aside to cool.

To assemble the trifle, pour a little custard onto the jelly in the serving dish. Dip two or three biscuits briefly in the extra sherry, place on the custard and sprinkle with a little marzipan. Spread over a little of the cooled jam mixture and top with some cooked cherries. Repeat the layering two or three times, finishing with a layer of custard. Cover with plastic film and refrigerate for a few hours, or preferably overnight.

Cut the remaining dish of jelly into small strips. To serve, top the trifle with whipped cream, jelly strips and extra cherries. Finish with the toasted almonds and icing sugar (if using).

SERVES 6

Choux pastry

200 ml water

200 ml milk

160 g unsalted butter

1½ teaspoons sugar

1 teaspoon pouring salt

240 g plain flour

6 large eggs

icing sugar, for dusting

Toffee sauce

120 g caster sugar

200 g thickened cream

75 g liquid glucose

1 teaspoon vanilla extract

25 g butter

Raisin cream filling

130 g raisins

100 ml brandy, warmed

3 tablespoons sugar

500 ml thickened cream

100 ml thick cream

80 g dark chocolate balls or chips

CHOUX RING WITH RAISIN CREAM AND TOFFEE SAUCE

This is very French, very rich and a great alternative to the traditional Christmas pudding.

Preheat the oven to 200°C (fan-forced). Line a baking tray with baking paper and draw a 20 cm circle in the centre.

To make the choux pastry, bring the water, milk, butter, sugar and salt to the boil in a saucepan over high heat. Add the flour and stir quickly with a wooden spoon until combined. Reduce the heat to medium and cook, stirring, for 10 minutes. Transfer the mixture to the bowl of an electric mixer with a paddle attachment.

In a separate bowl, whisk the eggs. Slowly add the eggs to the choux paste, mixing well between additions.

Spoon the paste into a piping bag with a 1 cm wide star nozzle. Pipe a 20 cm circle on the baking paper and then another inside (touching the first circle). Pipe a third circle on top, then pipe small decorative dots around the top.

Sprinkle the tray with a tablespoon of water (this helps the dough rise). Place the choux ring in the oven and bake for 5 minutes, then reduce the temperature to 165°C (fan-forced) and bake for 15–20 minutes or until brown and crisp. Remove and allow to cool. Use a serrated knife to slice off the top third and remove any wet dough inside. Set the choux ring aside.

For the toffee sauce, place the sugar in a saucepan over high heat and cook, without stirring, until the sugar melts and turns a caramel colour. Add the cream, glucose, vanilla and butter and bring to the boil, stirring constantly. Reduce the heat to low and simmer for 3–4 minutes. Pour into a lidded container and chill for at least 1 hour or until thickened.

Meanwhile, to make the filling, soak the raisins in the brandy for 20 minutes. Place the sugar and thickened cream in a bowl and whisk until thick. Fold in the thick cream. Roughly chop the raisins and fold half through the cream mixture with the brandy.

To assemble, fill the base of the pastry ring with the cream filling. Spoon over the toffee sauce, then scatter with the chocolate balls or chips and remaining raisins. Top with the lid and dust with icing sugar.

GLOSSARY

Baharat is a traditional Turkish spice blend that combines pepper with any or all of the following: paprika, cumin, coriander, cinnamon, cloves, cardamom, star anise and nutmeg. It is available from supermarkets and Middle Eastern shops.

Bottarga is the Italian word for dried, salt-cured mullet roe. Not surprisingly, it has an intense fish flavour that is almost sweet and salty at the same time. Available from fishmongers or speciality food shops in whole lobes or finely shaved or grated.

Bulgur (or burghul) is cracked wheat and comes in many grades, from fine to coarse. The wheat is boiled, then dried and ground to become bulgur. It is available from supermarkets and Middle Eastern shops.

Cavolo nero grows in long dark green stalks and can be picked very young and eaten raw in well-dressed salads, or picked later and cooked as a vegetable. It has a cabbage-like flavour and is also known as Tuscan kale.

Celery heart refers to the whole inner heart, usually comprising about four tightly packed, very pale celery sticks. The sticks and leaves are beautiful in salads.

Eggs are available in so many forms these days, but my preference is for free-range organic as the hens are well looked after and their eggs have the best flavour. If you can't get your hands on organic, look for free-range eggs from free-roaming chickens.

Fried shallots add a delightful crunch and caramelised-onion flavour to any dish – just sprinkle them over the top before serving. They are sold in Asian food stores or the Asian section of larger supermarkets.

Fromage frais and goat's curd are cheeses made from fresh, uncooked and unsalted curd. They have a short shelf-life, but their unique flavour and texture cannot be replaced with a cooked milk cheese. They are available at good cheese providores and delicatessens, but if you have trouble finding them, use a fresh ricotta or soft feta instead.

Gelatine is a neutral material used to 'set' foods. Available in powder and sheet form (I only use sheets), gelatine comes in varying strengths, graded as bronze, silver and gold. I use Alba gold leaf or Gelita gold leaf (both weigh 10 g for six sheets).

Grana padano is a younger and cheaper form of parmesan cheese. It has a sweeter, less sharp flavour so use it generously.

Harissa is an intense fiery paste made from red chillies, spices and a little salt. In my experience, the hottest variety comes from Tunisia. Look for it in delis, speciality food shops and larger supermarkets.

Horseradish is in season during the autumn and winter months. Buy fresh horseradish root, then peel and finely grate it before use. You can make do with the jarred version, but make sure you buy a brand that contains little or no sugar. It will not have the pungency of fresh horseradish, so you'll need to use a little more to get the same effect.

Liquid glucose is a thick, sweet syrup used as a sweetener in desserts, confectionery and other sweet foods. It is terrific in ice-cream as it has a low freezing point, which helps control the formation of sugar crystals. Corn syrup is similar and may be used in its place, if necessary.

Orange blossom water is water that has been infused with an extract of the blossom of orange trees. A heady, intense liquid commonly used in salads and desserts, and refreshing in cold lemon drinks and teas, it is available from specialist food stores and Middle Eastern and Greek delis.

Oven temperatures can vary significantly from oven to oven. I believe most people use fan-forced ovens these days so this is what I have given in the recipes – if you are using a conventional oven, set the temperature 10–20°C lower than stated in the recipes.

Palm sugar, also known as jaggery, is a sugar obtained from the sap of palm trees. I buy mine in a light to dark brown block and grate it as required, using the coarse side of a grater.

Pancetta is an Italian-style bacon. It is salt-cured pork belly, rolled tightly or curved flat, and sometimes spiced with dried chilli. Quality pancetta can be eaten like salami, sliced thickly for braises or thinly sliced and grilled to be eaten crisp in salads and soups.

Panko breadcrumbs are large, flaky breadcrumbs often used in Japanese cooking. The result is generally lighter and crispier than traditional breadcrumbs. They are available in supermarkets and Asian food stores.

Pecorino is a hard sheep's milk cheese (although cow's milk is sometimes added), produced in central and southern Italy. There are several different types of pecorino, each with a regional accent. I use Pecorino Romano in my recipes.

Pomegranate molasses is a concentrated pomegranate juice that has been reduced very slowly to create a sweet–sour syrup used sparingly in dressings and marinades. It should have a honey-like consistency. It is available from specialist and Middle Eastern shops.

Pomegranate seeds have a fruity, sweet flavour and a tart pip. Use them fresh in salads and desserts. To extract them, take a fresh pomegranate and cut through the red leathery skin to the honeycomb pith, where you will find the red jewel-like glassy seeds. Scoop these out with a spoon and remove the pith and membranes.

Ponzu sauce is soy sauce flavoured with citrus juice, vinegar, mirin, dashi stock and dried bonito flakes. It is often used as a dipping sauce or as part of a dressing.

Porcini powder, sometimes called 'kitchen tobacco', is used a lot in commercial kitchens. It's basically bits and pieces of dried porcini mushrooms ground into a powder. Available from speciality food stores, it's cheaper than buying whole porcini, and a couple of teaspoons will add an incredible depth of flavour to mushroom sauces and vegetable-based soups and braises.

Quinoa is an ancient grain that is highly nutritious and easy to digest. It has a wonderfully nutty flavour and may be used in soups, stews or salads. If you're unsure what to serve it with, just treat it like couscous or bulgur and you should be fine.

Saba is a type of sweet vinegar. Originally from southern Italy, this thick syrup is made by cooking the must (the unfermented juice from grapes that have been pressed to make wine) until the liquid is the consistency of honey. It is used as a condiment in dressings and drizzled over sweet and savoury food just before serving. It is available from Italian and specialist food stores.

Sea salt is a favourite of mine, as you can see from the recipes. I prefer to cook with sea salt flakes, but this is not essential. Use table salt if you like, but because it has a more intense flavour you will need to use less than the quantity stated in the recipes.

Shaoxing rice wine is a fermented rice wine commonly used in Chinese cooking. It has a similar flavour to dry sherry, and in fact you can use this as a substitute if necessary. Look for it in Asian food stores.

Tahini is a smooth paste made from ground white sesame seeds, with a little salt added. It is very intense, has a high oil content and will go rancid after it has been open for a couple of months. Keep it refrigerated.

Verjuice is made from unripened grapes, usually semillon or chardonnay. It has a more mellow flavour than lemon juice or wine vinegar, but can be used in place of these ingredients. It is available from delis and gourmet food stores.

Za'atar is a Middle Eastern spice blend of thyme, sesame seeds and sumac. It is available from spice shops and speciality stores. Sprinkle it over freshly cooked meats, fish or fried haloumi, over pita bread with oil before toasting, or add it to extra virgin olive oil for a quick dipping sauce to serve with bread.

ACKNOWLEDGEMENTS

This book is a miracle of sorts as it was written, tested and photographed at my home, which is chaotic at the best of times with two small children running around. But I'm hoping the warmth and clatter of a family home will really shine through, setting the scene for my recipes, which are all designed to share.

Thank you Stella and Amber for unpacking the fruit and veg for me so early in the morning. And Michael, thank you for your love, sense of humour and incredible patience. None of this would have been possible without your steady support.

To my father Pierre and meme Grace for tasting and enjoying the feast with us. Your smiles made me so proud.

To my dear mum Monica for being there in spirit – apologies for the timing, but there will be other books.

To Justine, Odette and Tony, thanks for your love and support, and being willing and able anytime. It was so special having you there.

Judy – again, it couldn't have happened so easily without you. You are a master of distraction and we love you so much.

Lemonia and Arthur, I just loved having you there for the Greek feast; and Tom and Elizabeth, thank you being so generous with your precious kitchen treasures

Thank you to my dear and talented chefs: Kylie, you did it again with ease and humour. I really enjoy working with you, my friend – you are a gun. Nicky, thank you for all your help from every angle. You are the perfect fit to our crazy team. And Ben, you are a master of a chef, and always ready to help out at the drop of a hat with professional expertise and patience.

A huge thank you to the wonderful kitchen teams at Melbourne Wine Room and Mr Wolf. You are all doing an amazing job, giving our restaurants a great and consistent reputation which enables me to do all the other stuff I love to do, such as write cookbooks!

Earl Carter – your photographic interpretation of my food is always exquisite. I just love working with the most professional photographer in the world. Thanks also to Wanda, Fraser and the rest of the team at Earl Carter Photography – you really get my food and I appreciate it more than I can say.

Thank you to my gorgeous friend Leesa O'Reilly. You helped me talk through my rough ideas with wine and laughter, and then brought it all to life with the most beautiful props, fabrics and surfaces.

Special thanks to Sam, John and the whole gang from Pinos at Prahran Market for their commitment to sourcing the freshest and best of all things in the fruit and vegetable department.

Julie Gibbs – the most lovely publisher ever – thank you for believing in the feasting direction and for always sharing the most intimate details of your latest cooking achievements.

A huge thank you to Ingrid Ohlsson, who seems to have all the time in the world to listen to me jabbering away about food and still manages to compile my thoughts into something I can be so proud of. And of course thank you to my editor Rachel Carter for so painstakingly adjusting every recipe, correction after correction, to make this book perfect.

Thanks also to the wonderful designers at Penguin who really pulled this book into line – Kirby Armstrong, Debra Billson, Megan Pigott and Daniel New. Finally, big thanks to Anyez Lindop, Sally Bateman and their crew for all the time and effort that goes into marketing the book.

INDEX

LANTERN

Published by the Penguin Group
Penguin Group (Australia)
250 Camberwell Road, Camberwell, Victoria 3124, Australia
(a division of Pearson Australia Group Pty Ltd)
Penguin Group (USA) Inc.
375 Hudson Street, New York, New York 10014, USA
Penguin Group (Canada)
90 Eglinton Avenue East, Suite 700, Toronto, Canada ON M4P 2Y3
(a division of Pearson Penguin Canada Inc.)
Penguin Books Ltd
80 Strand, London WC2R 0RL, England
Penguin Ireland
25 St Stephen's Green, Dublin 2, Ireland
(a division of Penguin Books Ltd)
Penguin Books India Pvt Ltd
11 Community Centre, Panchsheel Park, New Delhi – 110 017, India
Penguin Group (NZ)
67 Apollo Drive, Rosedale, North Shore 0632, New Zealand
(a division of Pearson New Zealand Ltd)
Penguin Books (South Africa) (Pty) Ltd
24 Sturdee Avenue, Rosebank, Johannesburg 2196, South Africa

Penguin Books Ltd, Registered Offices: 80 Strand, London,
WC2R 0RL, England

First published by Penguin Group (Australia), 2010

10 9 8 7 6 5 4 3 2 1

Design © Penguin Group (Australia)
Photography by Earl Carter
Styling by Leesa O'Reilly

Typeset in 11pt Adobe Garamond by Post Pre-press Group,
Brisbane, Queensland
Colour reproduction by Splitting Image, Clayton, Victoria
Printed and bound in China by Everbest Printing Co. Ltd.

National Library of Australia
Cataloguing-in-Publication data:

Martini, Karen.
Feasting / Karen Martini; photographer, Earl Carter.
9781921382352 (hbk.)
Includes index.
Cookery.
Other Authors/Contributors:
  Carter, Earl, 1957-

641.5

penguin.com.au

Thank you to the following stockists for sourcing
and providing props for our photo shoot:
Angelucci 20th Century (03) 9525 1271
Izzi & Popo (03) 9696 1771
Kris Coad 0403 918 719
Make Design Objects (03) 9347 4225
Manon Bis (03) 9521 1866
Market Import (03) 9500 0764
Moss Melbourne (03) 9525 5014
North Carlton Ceramics (03) 9347 2297
Safari Living (03) 9510 4500
The Essential Ingredient (03) 9827 9047
Trash On Bay (03) 9645 6511